FIVE SURVIVORS,
A HUNDRED LIVES

PEACEFUL IMPACT PUBLISHER
First English edition

The writers are five trauma survivors who all share the experience of living
with dissociative disorder.
Introduction: Anssi Leikola
Editor: Kaisa Klapuri
English translation: Kaija Anttonen
Proofreading: Michael Hurd
For further information about the book and the project, please see:
www.fivesurvivors.com

Graphic design: Carita Kilpinen CKV.fi & Seija Hirstiö, Heartwaves Design
Cover and cover art: Carita Kilpinen
All artwork in this book is produced by the survivors.
Print Hansaprint Ltd, Turku, 2017

ISBN 978-952-7203-02-6

If you wish to purchase copies of the book, please visit the following website
for information on how to order: www.fivesurvivors.com
or contact@fivesurvivors.com

FIVE SURVIVORS, A HUNDRED LIVES

Stories about Trauma and Dissociation

Peaceful Impact

PUBLISHER

TABLE OF CONTENTS

About the authors   7
Foreword   9
Introduction by Anssi Leikola   16
Kaisa Klapuri   55
Inari Heikkilä   86
Carita Kilpinen   98
Seija Hirstiö   156
Epilogue   208
Bibliography   214

Artwork by Carita

INTRODUCTION OF THE AUTHORS

Anssi Leikola is a 52-year-old man and a psychiatrist who, among other professional activities, trains psychotherapists. He has the exceptional skill of being able to empathise with people who are living in what can be described as hell on earth. This skill has been refined through his experience of living for decades with a personality that was structurally divided (i.e., dissociated) and through the process of becoming whole, and it can now be used collectively and for the benefit of society. Anssi's mission to promote the situation of traumatised people began in the early 2000s, but only now does he feel that he has found a community in which he can feel coequal in a completely new way. Today he has two adult children and lives in a happy relationship based on equality.

Kaisa Klapuri, 35, was born in Finland but lives now in Sweden, where she works as a language teacher. She loves horses and cats, writing and reading, and colourful clothes and sweets. Kaisa was raised in a small Christian congregation and experienced sexual abuse as a child. She has dissociative identity disorder, which was, in her youth, mistakenly diagnosed as schizophrenia, with disastrous results.

Inari Heikkilä, 33, is a practical nurse and the mother of a teenage girl. She receives a disability pension, but is also studying at present. Skydiving and teaching skydiving are her passions. Inari had to live with physical violence, subjugation, isolation and sexual abuse in her childhood. She has dissociative identity disorder.

Carita Kilpinen is a 35-year-old mother of two children; she is also an entrepreneur and artist who loves animals, being in the forest and doing things with her hands, as well as everything that has to do with nature. Recurring incidents of traumatisation that began early in her life have caused her to suffer from a difficult dissociative disorder. After twelve years of trauma therapy, Carita has now reached the terminal point of her therapeutic journey. From now on, she intends to enjoy life and continue writing stories.

Seija Hirstiö, 54, is a media designer, documentarist and the mother of a child. Her traumas were caused by childhood abuse and neglect. She has travelled a 20-year-long road to healing, and is grateful for the work she has been able to do together with body and trauma psychotherapists. Seija has written an earlier book called *Trauma1* and was also the initiator of this book project. She wanted to create a dissociation community so that as many people as possible could win back their strength and zest for life, share their stories and become active people who can have an impact.

FOREWORD

The authors' experiences of the journey

Seija:

Our books – printed and digital books in Finnish, as well as this English version – have been born as a result of coincidental meetings, without planning. There is nothing very usual in the way they have come about, which is exactly why our project has been so powerful and constructive. We are creating a new view that will empower trauma survivors on the long and demanding road towards healing.

I launched the project by hanging around in Internet chat rooms, asking whether there were people who would be willing to participate in writing a book about their traumatisation and dissociative disorder together with me. In the beginning, there was one other person who was daring enough, and, after a year, there were five of us who had managed to stick to the project, while many people had left soon after joining the group.

It's not easy to write a book about your own dissociative disorder. We divided the writing process into parts, and set a goal for each month. This provided the necessary structure for our writing. We live in different parts of Finland, which means that we were physically alone during the writing.

At regular intervals, someone would disappear from the group, but was found or came back later, sometimes even after a period of several months. During the process, some people fell seriously ill or spent long periods on wards; there were suicide attempts and general dissociative symptoms. We did our best to care for each other genuinely and encouraged each other to keep fighting. "Don't hurt yourself!" was a common wish expressed when we were chatting.

There were times when I didn't know whether to cry or laugh. Since the memory of people with dissociative disorders works in an atypical way, the writers kept asking things like "Now where are those instructions again?" and "What was I was supposed to do now?" In the beginning, one of us might suddenly wonder who a certain member of the group actually was.

For me, the most important thing was to be able to push the project ahead by concentrating on the essential: the thought of how empowering it is for a traumatised person to write his or her own story and participate in confidential cooperation. Therefore, occasional phases of self-destructiveness or fading interest never became overriding issues during the project. We just carried on, and, after a few years, we had enough stories, photos, paintings and videos for an e-edition of our book. The title of our first book was *Viisi naista, sata elämää* ("Five Women, a Hundred Lives").

For me, another important goal of our project from the very beginning was to create an ethical working culture: for example, we would never intentionally hurt each other. I felt that, to build up trust, we needed to be especially considerate towards each other. We also agreed that if anyone in the group was opposed to a new idea, we would not follow through with it or insist on discussing the issue in any way.

We soon realised that our group had a variety of skills: we had authors who wrote prose or poetry, artists who drew, photographers and video makers, musicians, dancers, language professionals and bloggers. With time, the authors began, quite naturally, to assume responsibility for the parts of the book that they felt they could work on. We had no funding, so making use of all our skills was both empowering and a prerequisite for carrying out the project.

The book you now hold in your hands is part of the second phase of our project. In this English version, we have a new author, Carita Kilpinen; Anssi Leikola, who participated earlier only as an expert on dissociative disorder, now also writes as a person who has himself suffered from dissociative disorder. Our aim is that our project will keep growing and changing.

We have built up new awareness among traumatised people by publishing our own website www.dissociation.fi, by writing a blog that is updated regularly and by having an open Facebook page. On these digital platforms, we have managed to engage many guest writers, from trauma survivors to health professionals. The most intense feelings I've had during this project of many years are feelings of success and gratitude.

For a long time, I have tried to find new writers and people who would be willing to share responsibility for the project. But traumatised people must find their own motivation for this kind of activity. Gradually, we are achieving our goal, and interest in our project is increasing. It's delightful to notice that, for most of the survivors, it is important to be able to contribute to a change that will hopefully make the treatment of dissociative disorder in psychiatry more humane and the comprehensive treatment of trauma more common.

Our book project can provide a platform for publishing digital books globally (VOB e-book), and one of our goals is to enable traumatised people to publish their stories easily and safely. We also have a publishing house of our own – something for which we can thank the founder, Jukka Turunen, and Anssi Leikola, who provided the funding. We provide training in managing a group process and creating texts, images and videos.

This is a good time to be visible and do away with the stigma that is easily attached to people who are recovering from mental health issues! The human mind constructs the future on the basis of earlier experiences and views, and therefore, the public image of mental health problems changes slowly. We traumatised people have to show the way to a new reality on our own, drawing upon our views and the strength within us. Trauma is a loss, but it also offers the possibility to create something new.

I would like to extend my deepest thanks and love to my amazing daughter Petra and my loving partner Jukka.

Seija Hirstiö, designer, documentarist, author

Kaisa:
When I saw on Facebook in 2013 that Seija was looking for writers for a book on dissociative disorder, I immediately decided to participate. At that point, I wasn't actually thinking of telling my story to the readers: I

merely wanted to find peers through the project. And I did: with time, all the authors of the book became my friends. Little by little, I grew braver and felt a stronger desire to come out with my past and thus help other people who had gone through similar experiences.

By helping others, I have also helped myself. Not everything in this world has a purpose at the beginning, but we can always work at creating a purpose. During this project, many people have told me that our stories have helped them find out what happened in their past and what is wrong with them. Many people have also begun to believe in the possibility of healing. Because of this response, it was worth the effort to write about myself in the book, though coming out has been a difficult experience in many ways. In the English edition of our book, I have decided to use my real name. Truth liberates.

I feel that talking about trauma and dissociation is especially important because it can contribute to a gradual change in the practices of psychiatric treatment. I banged my head against the system for years, while the psychiatric treatment I received crushed my joy and zest for life and actually prevented me from recovering. In a way, my heart is still on a closed ward: I almost cry every time I remember my friends who are now on those wards, half-dead, mute and with no strength – all because of the treatment they are receiving. I would give anything to be able to offer them a possibility, a voice. Mental health problems are one of the last big taboos in our society.

In future, I want to participate in writing new books and creating peer groups for people suffering from dissociative disorder. I'm also interested in trauma research. As strange as it may sound, the special skills that dissociative people have include the ability to read thoughts and feelings and predict the future. I'm an extremely rational person, but there have been times when I haven't been able to explain the special kind of sensitivity dissociative people have. A child or a young person who grows up in fear of violence and abuse has to be extremely attuned to their environment and develop instincts and senses with which to interpret it. Learning more about this sensitivity would be an interesting future project.

I would never have made it without friends, peers, and loved ones. Thank you. I dedicate my story to the Psychiatric Unit 16 in Kokkola.

Kaisa Klapuri, language teacher, author

Inari:

When I decided to participate in our Finnish book on dissociation a few years ago my condition was very different from what it is now. I had a full-time disability pension and I was struggling with both physical and mental problems. I was self-destructive; I felt hopeless and ended up several times in life-threatening situations. I was in a wheelchair and it seemed that life had little to offer me. It was difficult for me to be in the here and now and to understand my life, and, indeed, I managed to finish my text for the book only at the last moment.

My situation is very different now that we are about to publish our book in English. I have returned to studying and working, and I can walk – and even roller skate – on my own two feet! Rehabilitation from the dissociative disorder still takes a large part of my resources, but I no longer feel hopeless.

This situation is the result of therapy and an improvement in my physical condition, but also our book project and dissociative community. I have found friends who understand me, and I have started to get a good overall picture of my life and my disease. This project has empowered me, making me feel that my life has meaning and I can achieve something. I am not a hopeless case after all!

I would like to thank my friends, the members of my dissociative group and my therapist with all my heart.

Inari Heikkilä

Carita:

Slightly more than a year ago I was visiting a book fair, anxious and excited. When surfing the Web, I had come across a book called *Viisi naista, sata elämää* ["Five Women, a Hundred Lives"], and now I had a chance to buy the book for myself at the fair. I was, of course, extremely interested in the book, but, above all, I looked forward to meeting people like me face to face. Meeting them was definitely an impressive experience. I went home with the book under my arm, and immediately sat down to write my first guest text in the blog dissociation.fi. This meant that I had "come out of the closet" with my story, visibly and intentionally. The coming out happened very suddenly, but, by that time, I had been processing the issue for years. It was time. I haven't regretted my decision for a moment!

I got a huge number of positive responses, and when I was asked to be one of the authors of a new book, I didn't hesitate. In half a year, I did something I never thought I could do: I wrote, intentionally, a life story dozens of pages long. The process completely changed my life.

Working with peers – people who belong to the same tribe – has been an experience from which I've learned incredibly much. I'm impressed by the strength and determination in this small book community of ours. Despite our heavy loads, we get things done.

Through working with peers, I've found the last missing piece in the puzzle of my life that I've persistently worked on in therapy for the past twelve years. The book has helped me find myself, my way back to people, and my mission.

I dedicate my part of this book to my beloved, kind, brave and strong older brother, who has found the strength to be empathetic and gentle towards me, despite his own heavy load.
Thank you, Sami Ketola – my Brother Lionheart.

Carita Kilpinen, entrepreneur, graphic designer, artist

Artwork by Carita

INTRODUCTION

Anssi Leikola
Psychiatrist, therapist, author, trauma survivor

This book marks an important milestone in the change that is taking place in psychiatry. It consists of stories about the effects of unbearable experiences in the childhood development phase: that is, stories about trauma and dissociative disorders. They are stories that are all too often neither told nor heard nor understood.

The real nature of these mental health disorders, which are always linked with serious emotional damage, often remains unclear even for professionals engaged in the field of psychiatry. The dissociative identity disorder (DID), for example, has often been mystified; even its very existence has been called into question from time to time. Our book offers readers the opportunity to understand the nature of dissociative disorders and identify with experiences that have hardly ever been presented in Finnish literature. It is highly probable that psychiatry is moving towards focusing more on emotional traumatisation as the cause of mental disorders.

Interest in dissociative disorders has clearly increased in Finland in recent years. Nevertheless, dissociative disorders still play a marginal role in everyday diagnostics compared to the more well-established disorder groups of contemporary psychiatry. The exact meaning of the concept of "dissociation" is still unclear. There are many questions in the air, with no precise answers. What does the word actually mean? How is it connected with traumas? What is a trauma, or a traumatising experience in life? In terms of these questions, too, this book is a significant and authentic source of information. It will increase our knowledge, leading to an understanding that will change attitudes.

The word "dissociation" has become a confusing term as different people mean different things by it. It is rapidly becoming a new buzzword in psychiatry, one which is still used rather loosely. I have studied the subject extensively since the beginning of the 2000s, arguing that the term should have a more precise meaning than it has in its official definition (Leikola, 2014). Despite these semantic challenges, the concept of "dissociation" seems to be essential when we try to understand a traumatised person comprehensively, looking for the truth. We must avoid fruitless disagreement concerning the correct definition of the term. Thus, this introduction is not intended to prove that my way of seeing the issue is the only truth. Nevertheless, the problem of defining dissociation is crucial in one respect: in my experience, the failure to agree on a definition may prevent a genuine meeting between people if they are not actually talking about the same thing. At worst, words can become an obstacle to mutual understanding and sharing that heals.

According to Daniel Stern, one of the most essential factors in psychotherapy is the experience of meeting, which he calls "the moment of meeting" (Stern, 2004). This means that there is a mutually shared experience and state of consciousness in interactions between people in which both parties simultaneously grasp and experience the same thing and are also aware of their identical experiences. Stern considers these precise moments as corrective and healing in psychotherapy, as well as in life in general. I have also had the experience that this kind of sharing is life-changing. This book provides the possibility of meeting in an atmosphere of security between the writers and the readers.

Anssi Leikola
psychiatrist, therapist,
author, trauma survivor

ABOUT THE AUTHOR

The views presented in this introduction are based on a multidisci-plinary survey of literature and my own experience in treating numer-ous trauma patients and following their healing processes intensively over long periods of time. I have met people with dissociative disorders and those treating them while working as a psychiatrist, therapist, work supervisor and lecturer. On the other hand, my views are also based on my own experiences as a patient.

To make one thing immediately clear, I have not been involved in treating the other authors of this book, with one exception: I treated one of them almost a decade ago – and only briefly. When I became involved in this book project in the autumn of 2015, I did not know the authors; I had never even met three of them. Yet their stories immediately sound-ed familiar to me in terms of trauma history, symptoms, problems and experiences of treatment.

A mental disorder connected with trauma follows a universal pat-tern; this kind of pattern can also be seen in the stories of this book, and has been experienced as personal and meaningful by the people who wrote these stories. One of the important flashes of insight into what dissociation is revolutionised my own life in 2001. It happened when I was being treated at the Lapinlahti Psychiatric Clinic in Helsinki. I now know that it was the moment when, for the first time, I became aware of how it feels when one part of the personality gives way to another part. At that point, I did not yet understand what was happening as analyti-cally as I do now, but I did grasp the importance of the experience and the fact that I had found my mission in life. On the ward, we never really reached an understanding concerning my condition and experiences: I eventually felt that my views were, at the very least, being ignored and overruled by the use of more traditional diagnoses. Fortunately, how-ever, the communication and interaction between me and my personal nurse and music therapist was safe and crucially valuable.

A completely new connection was born inside me.

The dramatic effect of these experiences has been manifested by the fact that I have not suffered from a single dissociative psychosis following that period of hospitalisation (cf. Van der Hart et al., 2008). This means that these vital experiences, their successful sharing, and the understanding and realisation with which they were connected changed the structure of my personality, as well as my life, in a remarkable and permanent way.

I am convinced that if the trauma aetiology of my mental problems and the dissociated structure of my personality had been understood earlier, I would not have needed such a long period – altogether over sixteen years – of psychotherapy aimed at the integration of my personality.

Although I am a man and have never been a victim of sexual abuse, identifying with the other authors of this book has changed me, once again. My trauma was caused by early neglect in particular. Each life story is individual and unique, but there are also fixed consequences that can be generalised. The fact that these fixed patterns of structural dissociation have a crucial meaning in everyday life also means that they can and should be studied and verified scientifically. They offer us the possibility of mutual identification. This kind of approach is still rare at present, but probably will not be rare much longer.

It has been important for me to realise how my stronger sense of security, in addition to my increasing cognitive understanding and work experience, has clearly improved the effect of treatment. As a sign of this, several patients of mine are now on the threshold of personality integration: they have come to terms with the totality of their life stories, and the unbearable emotions of the past have been worked through – have become realised – profoundly enough as the result of an enormous amount of work and a series of successful meetings and sharing; the experiences now have their own place in these people's histories, and the trauma-related core beliefs concerning the self have gradually been transformed. For a few patients, the work has been completed and the personality has become sufficiently integrated, and both parties have agreed that there is no longer any need for visits. For most of my patients, however, the realistic goal is that the process will move gradually towards the structural integration of the personality. I bear the responsibility for and am committed to achieving this goal. It is always a long

A completely new
connection inside

process, but I believe I know what it will take.

In terms of trauma therapy, it is good to live in Finland, because the psychotherapeutic treatment culture seems to be more advanced here than in many other European countries. This is mainly a result of the internationally recognised training which has been offered in Finland for a long time – and from which I myself have benefited so much. The treatment of dissociative disorders is a hundred-year-old tradition, and its pioneers, bearers and messengers – experts in trauma psychotherapy and sensorimotor psychotherapy – have regularly trained, supervised and educated us Finnish experts in this demanding profession (see, e.g., Steele et al., 2005; Van der Hart et al., 2006; Ogden et al., 2006; Boon et al., 2012; Nijenhuis, 2015 & 2017). Trauma therapy has gained an exceptionally central position and can now even be considered one of the main trends of psychotherapy in Finland (Poijula et al., 2015).

However, at this point there are very few psychiatrists specialised in treating trauma and, in particular, in treating structural dissociation in Finland. Medication often plays an important role in the treatment of emotional trauma, but, unfortunately, medicine can also prevent healing sometimes. Thus, it is a great advantage if the psychiatrist has extensive knowledge of the treatment of dissociative disorders and is familiar with the healing process. Cooperation between the psychotherapist and psychiatrist has proved to be beneficial if the patient, in addition to going to therapy, meets a psychiatrist at longer but regular intervals. This brings an increased sense of overall security to psychotherapy-oriented treatment, facilitating and speeding up the process of healing.

As a scientific starting-point, the recognition of the importance of trauma is becoming increasingly common in psychiatry in many countries. As recently as twenty years ago this was seldom the case. In practical psychiatry in Finland, the linkage between trauma and dissociation is gradually gaining a foothold, though the trend has not yet made sufficient headway in the sphere of science. When I was writing my book *Katkennut totuus* ("The Broken Truth", 2014), I ran head-on into a conflict between established and more modern ways of thinking: it was not possible to write a doctoral thesis on my material due to its cross-disciplinary, philosophical and holistic nature. Perhaps it was also too transformational.

Psychiatry (and medicine) is dominated by a certain "thought style" – a term coined by social psychologist Ludwik Fleck (1935) when he reflected on the impact of social factors in science. As concerns scientific progress, there is one major obstacle: the fact that the original concept of "dissociation", so essential for successful treatment, is clearly based on a different thought style. Following Fleck's thinking, the crucial thing is how a "thought collective" that shares this kind of fresh thought style can emerge. Another crucial point is that, with such a new thought style, we get completely new scientific facts (see also Siwecka, 2011). It seems that a subculture based on this "deviant" approach has already been created. As we will soon notice here, creating real understanding of traumas and their treatment requires philosophical vigilance.

The thought style that is connected with structural dissociation has had extremely positive effects for me when I've worked on the puzzles of my life. Through this writing, I try to tell about these effects to the reader. To put it simply, dissociation is then not just a symptom: it is a structure. A structure that produces symptoms and many other effects. If we can't see this basic conceptual incommensurability and recognise its fundamental meaning and impact, scientific discussion may turn into band-aid discussion. Then, there will be no genuine meeting between the parties, and it will, once more, be the traumatised person who suffers.

Little by little, however, there will be a change in psychiatric thought, and we will approach a more comprehensive and, actually, more biological form of psychiatry in which the goal is healing and transforming structure, not just the management of symptoms.

Phenomenologist Edmund Husserl's idea that being ethical means transformation speaks to me profoundly (Husserl, 1924). I have frequently had the experience that healing and integration lead to transformation. Today, I have compassion for myself when it comes to my incompleteness, lack of understanding and limited abilities. I can provide background support and serve as an example for many, and I can enjoy what I have.

WHAT IS DISSOCIATION?

Pierre Janet (1859–1947) created his basic theories on dissociation as early as the 1800s in a French tradition in which the connection between traumatisation and mental disorders was widely recognised and accepted (Van der Kolk & Van der Hart, 1989). He developed a valuable theoretical frame of reference and a treatment model for healing traumas.

Etymologically, the word "trauma" means "damage" or "wound". Even professionals often mix things up, and "trauma" is quite commonly used to refer to an experience or event in a person's life. However, "trauma" should be used to refer specifically to the emotional damage an event has caused in a person. This becomes much simpler if, in looking for a definition, we return to Pierre Janet's ideas. "Emotional trauma" refers to psychophysical damage manifested as a splitting of the personality.

It is also essential that the concept of "structural dissociation" is understood precisely and internalised. Countless authors and professionals use the term "dissociation" in different, contradictory and/or ambiguous ways. Furthermore, the official definition of dissociation is too vague in disorder classifications, and I am not the only one who has this opinion. In this book – as in the field of trauma treatment in general – this word is used in diverse ways. For me, it means precisely the splitting of one's personality: that is, structural dissociation. I will now try to express in a simplified way what this means in practice.

Structural dissociation is manifested in such a way that, in connection with traumatisation, one's personality becomes split into parts that experience both themselves and the world in different ways. The personality becomes divided into at least two parts as the result of an unbearable emotional state that has a powerful and paralysing effect on one's capacity to act. One of the two parts of the personality consists of a defensive reaction triggered by a life-threatening situation and traumatic memories of it; it is called the "emotional part of personality" (the EP). The other part is characterised by an effort to continue living as if the damaging experience had never occurred; it is called the "apparently normal part of personality" (the ANP). This splitting of the personali-

Artwork by Anssi

The Beacon
Lights Have
Disappeared

ty in response to severe psychological damage seems to be the original meaning of "dissociation" – a meaning I have absorbed while following in the footsteps of Pierre Janet and Professor Onno van der Hart.

In the spirit of Janet, we can say that emotional trauma is a failure in the process of synthesising one's personality. There is no cause-and-effect relationship between trauma and dissociation: they are the same thing, though expressed in different terms.

Structural dissociation is the most important common denominator uniting the stories of this book. Still, the stories are all different, just as every life story is different. Adopting the original meaning of the concept of dissociation may increase both the concept's explanatory value and its consistent use in everyday work with patients.

At best, this rather simple definition can be shared by professionals and patients alike and will, in that case, guide daily practical work on traumatisation. This means that a traumatised person will finally feel that he or she is seen as a whole being: that is, the various parts of his/her personality are gradually met and taken into consideration and their invaluable message is understood in therapy.

As I understand it, dissociation – and structural dissociation to be precise – was Janet's single most important concept. This view is supported both by the countless shared moments of insight I have had in treating traumatised people, and by my own experience of healing. Indeed, Janet's theory on the structural dissociation of the personality has helped me grasp in a completely new way what traumatisation and its effects are all about, what kind of approach is needed to analyse and understand the life of a traumatised person, and how the person can be treated. Onno van der Hart and his colleagues have been concerned with the meaning of "dissociation" for a long time, speaking in favour of a consistent meaning for the concept all over the world.

The same basic division (ANP – EP) can also be found in post-traumatic stress disorders (PTSD). However, it is manifested in a clearer and more complex form in dissociative identity disorders (DID). The set of symptoms displayed by a traumatised person is explained by a characteristic and dynamic alternating pattern between the different parts of the personality. Professionals working with traumas have been familiar

Artwork by Anssi

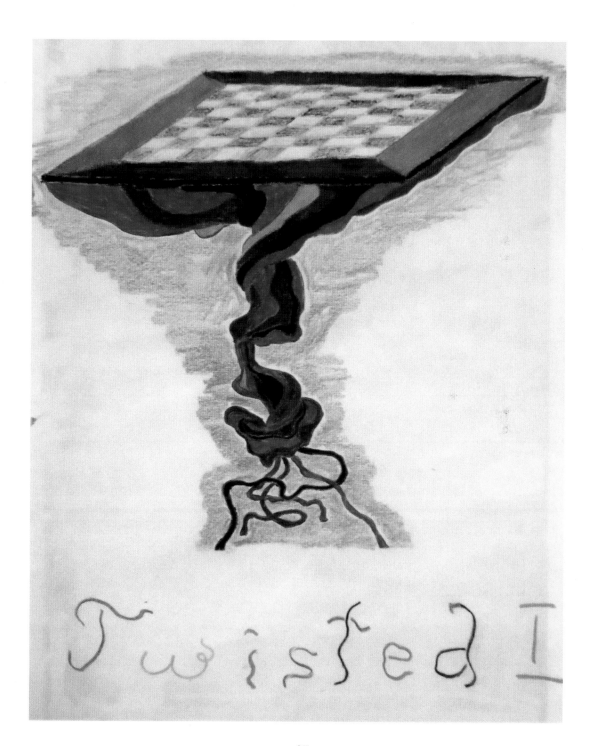

Twisted produces a flower

with this alternation for at least 150 years. I have examined the surprisingly diverse implications of this relatively simple phenomenon and its effect on psychiatry in my book Katkennut totuus.

The theory of traumatisation is a construct that is continuously evolving. A great indication of this is the trinity model introduced by Ellert Nijenhuis in his recent book Trinity of Trauma (2015 & 2017), in which EPs can be divided into two main categories, fragile and controlling EPs. In its simplicity, Nijenhuis's redefinition is ingenious and immediately applicable to practice. When the light dawns on both therapist and patient, the expressions on their faces cannot be misinterpreted.

I could even claim that a traumatised person cannot be understood wholly and sufficiently without the concept of structural dissociation. Still, it is equally essential to remember that every person is unique. We should not make the mistake of trying to be prescient.

We reach a completely new level of understanding of the stories of this book – and of all life stories dealing with a variety of emotional injuries – when they are analysed using the two most important theories concerning trauma treatment. The first is the theory on the structural dissociation of the personality described earlier. The other is the polyvagal theory, which explains how the autonomic nervous system works and how people defend themselves when threatened. Since a sense of security is the most important condition for healing, I consider it an enormous advance that we now understand how the autonomic nervous system works in therapeutic relationships. The capacity of the autonomic nervous system to act is shaped by experiences, which explains why traumatised people often have distinct problems defending themselves properly (Leikola et al., 2016). As gestalt therapist Kurt Lewin has wisely noted, "Nothing is as practical as a good theory". Here we have at least two of them.

In addition to structural dissociation, traumatised people sometimes experience a range of "altered states of consciousness". This applies to people with severe childhood traumas in particular. These altered states of consciousness aim at the same thing as the structural dissociation of the personality: non-realisation, as opposite to realisation. Alterations of consciousness can equally well mean a narrowed field or lowering of

Artwork by Anssi

the level of consciousness. Typically, they are manifested in practice in such a way that the person does not feel the present environment very much, or an outsider feels that the person has partly vanished or can no longer even be contacted. The reactions are, in a way, subconscious ways of avoiding the knowledge of what has happened in the past, what the experience means, and how it has affected one's life (Van der Hart et al., 2004).

Thus, the organism has, in the course of evolution, acquired many ways of avoiding awareness of harmful experiences of the past. But the cost of such avoidance is high, as all the contributors to this book show in an analytical way. Sometimes such intense altered states of consciousness are also referred to using the term "dissociation", although they are clearly different phenomena than the structural dissociation of the personality.

There is infinite variation in the manifestations and depths of the structural dissociation of the personality and in the relations between the parts of the personality. On the other hand, due to the basic biological structure of human beings, we can expect to find certain characteristic parts of the personality. Mechanisms, or emotional operating systems, that are common to all mammals (see, e.g., Panksepp, 1998) guide human behaviour both in ordinary situations and in situations where we are defending ourselves against danger. What it all boils down to is how integrated – and thus cooperative – these mechanisms are.

TREATMENT AND RECOGNISING DISSOCIATION

Adopting a trauma approach in the practices and guidelines of psychiatric treatment leads to new kinds of built-in empathy, humanity and mercifulness, all of which have intrinsic value as part of the main mission of psychiatry. The life stories presented in this book demonstrate repeatedly what an essential role the diagnosis of a dissociative disorder has had for us authors. Our lives have changed radically after the frame of reference of traumatisation and dissociation was adopted as the starting point of treatment. A new basis for understanding was achieved, providing a decisive push towards corrective and psychotherapeutic treatment. I have repeatedly witnessed a similar development in my own practice. To a great extent, progress has often been the result of finally being seen, heard and understood the way you are, warts and all. In such a situation, the possibility for successful moments of meeting increases beyond measure. There is a whole new basis for the growth of motivation and trust in treatment and therapy.

Healing psychotherapeutic treatment must aim at a situation where the main points of the real story with all its meanings are gradually told, genuinely understood, put in proportion, and shared. In order to achieve this, we must cooperate with the whole person. This is part of Janet's treatment model in which a satisfactory amount of a certain type of successful mental activity eventually affects the structures of the personality. This means that a large number of personal experiences of realisation leads to structural changes in the personality, eventually making profound healing possible (more about this in the section on Realisation). The main pre-condition for realisation is the creation of a sense of security, which should be the guiding principle of all treatment.

THE TRAUMA SPECTRUM

The spectrum of trauma-related disorders reaches far and wide. In this book the focus is on complex dissociative disorders, in which the personality is divided in intricate ways and the parts of the personality may have become differentiated and independent. However, most of the basic principles of trauma treatment can be applied to all levels of traumatisation: that is, to the effects of all experiences in which the intensity of an emotion surpasses the tolerance of the individual at a given moment. In order to cope with extreme experiences, we need other people. Without them, we cannot integrate these experiences into the rest of our life stories.

The spectrum of traumatic experiences reveals something important about the overall picture. I am currently responsible for the treatment of about fifty patients, as either a therapist or a psychiatrist. Concerning the causes of emotional damage, I can say, on the basis of my experience

The Relationship
with the Mother

with these patients, that traumas are closely connected with sexual violence in probably less than half of the cases. Thus, for the majority of my clients, the traumas are linked to something else: for example, physical violence, failed attachment (insufficient or distorted parenting), childhood neglect, emotional abuse, bullying, traumatic loss, painful sickness or frightening hospital experiences in childhood. Each injury type has its own characteristics, but there are also many similarities. The structural dissociation of the personality can very well be caused by a multitude of unbearable experiences. The conditions of childhood development can be unsafe in diverse ways, with the past of an individual often containing various combinations of the circumstances listed above.

Traumatic experiences in childhood lead to incomplete coherence of the personality. The normal development of the personality is hindered, with development taking a different path. Traumatisation, and especially retraumatisation, can also occur after the childhood events, even when the person is already an adult. Unfortunately, this also happens in connection with failures, shortcomings and even malpractice in psychiatric treatment. To an astonishing extent, it is the result of the practitioner (or health care system) not being able to recognise this – typically hidden – damage. The therapeutic curing process is essentially complicated if the patient has been traumatised not only in childhood but also at some point during treatment by a psychiatrist or psychotherapist.

Nevertheless, there is something good in everyone's background: in order to understand the whole picture and rebuild the history of the person, it is also necessary to be aware of the secure, protective and healing experiences and relationships the patient has had.

It is hardly ever possible for an individual to heal from childhood traumas without proper help from a professional specialised in the treatment of traumatisation. Treatment is necessary in particular if the experiences are hidden and deeply embedded in different parts of the personality, and the beliefs concerning the trauma have already strongly shaped the person's way of living. We, the authors of this book, are at various stages of healing, and, as can be seen from our texts, we have come a long way. For all of us writers, participation in this book has entailed quite a leap forward in the personal healing and growth processes.

33

Artwork by Anssi

In the cure of traumatisation, it is essential to understand that integration does not occur in an even, linear fashion: there can be dramatic, lasting changes. On the other hand, the activation of traumatic memories often gives rise to the feeling of returning to the starting-point, and that is when the memories of earlier experiences of healing and success may temporarily be forgotten or seem to evaporate into thin air.

In the life stories in this book, we can also find accounts of substantial disturbances in the sense of reality, as many traumatised people suffer from symptoms that have traditionally been characterised as psychotic. Though there will no doubt be loud protests, it is justified to say that emotional traumatisation probably explains a majority of the psychot-

sometimes
trauma
transforms
itself
from
generation
to another..

34

Artwork by Anssi

ic symptoms we habitually treat with medication. Finnish researchers dealing with psychosis are also beginning to reach the conclusion that there is a significant connection between traumatisation and psychosis (Hietala et al., 2015). There is also extensive, indisputable evidence for this connection in international research (e.g., Schäfer et al., 2008; Read et al., 2014). Similarly, depression – the Finnish "national disease" – can be meaningfully examined from the point of view of trauma, both empirically/epigenetically (e.g., Caspi et al., 2003) and theoretically (Huttunen & Leikola, 2017). These are excellent examples of the measure of change in which psychiatry now finds itself. Time will show how the impact of this dramatic change is reflected in the diagnostic system itself. What is a sensible way of classifying psychological disorders? It is a difficult question, but it must be asked.

To my mind, no childhood trauma can be considered mild, as it would be unfair – as far as I can tell on the basis of my experience as a witness. This is the case at least in my office. Emotional injury is always a serious issue, involving especially painful experiences and requiring a great deal from treatment. There are people with various kinds of severe injuries who have often had to live for years or decades in difficult circumstances and go through unbearable feelings. The effect of traumatisation steers one's life and choices to a great extent. Past experiences are manifested and often continue as a hidden inner drama in which the roles are played by separate parts of the personality. Occasionally, this also becomes apparent externally, on the level of detectable symptoms and behaviour. The process is especially clear with the dissociative identity disorder, but once again, the manifestations of the disorder are usually carefully hidden.

A practitioner needs an experienced eye and a safe mind to be able to read and build a life story from the symptoms, behaviour and verbal allusions of the patient – a story that is constantly and repeatedly being complemented and consolidated. As the stories of this book show, we are talking about a regular, long-term project lasting for years. Such a long time span does not seem very fashionable in our hectic, instantaneous Western culture, which is impatient, avoids commitment and shuns all dependency (cf. Steele et al., 2001). However, there is no shortcut.

Transgenerational
Shame

DISSOCIATIVE IDENTITY DISORDER (DID)

I have treated several patients with dissociative identity disorder as a psychiatrist or therapist. As a supervisor, I have also met with, listened to, witnessed and shared dozens of other life stories and treatment processes linked with this disorder. In doing so, I have gained some experience in recognising the characteristics of DID patients' special problems and effective treatment processes for dealing with them. A clear majority (perhaps as many as 80 per cent) of the patients I have treated represent types of traumatisation other than DID. Structurally, their personalities are not as divided as those of DID patients. The dissociative identity disorder represents the most complex disorder of the trauma spectrum, but its diagnostic criteria are not completely unambiguous, either; thus, there are also in-between cases (see, e.g., Nijenhuis, 2015, minor DID vs. major DID).

Thanks to the use of the best technology, the existence of dissociative parts of the personality has been proven scientifically. The evidence is based on both functional magnetic imaging (fMRI) and positron emission tomography (PET images). Studies have been done on DID patients in particular, imaging their brain activity in suitable, carefully arranged experimental tests. For example, these studies have had control groups consisting of actors who have been directed to act as parts of a personality (e.g., Reinders et al., 2006; Schlumpf et al., 2014).

By now, we also have preliminary research results even on how to measure the healing process in the brain of a DID patient. The effect of healing is visible in the volume of the hippocampus and the area around it. It is a special part of the brain, as it combines the past and the present, integrating memories and experiences (Ehling et al., 2008). This is possible because neurogenesis, the birth of new nerve cells, goes on in the hippocampus throughout one's life – unlike in the brain in general.

We can well ask whether there is evidence that is as impressive and as psychobiologically specific for any other psychiatric disorder as we now have for dissociative identity disorder! This psychobiological disorder and its tertiary structural dissociation are the logically and scientifically understandable effects of unbearable experiences.

Artwork by Anssi

Dissociative amnesia – the inability to remember – can also occur in many other trauma-related disorders, but it is often striking in DID. It may cause special problems that need to be taken into consideration in treatment. This kind of special, psychologically understandable memory disorder, which tends to hide but appears in dynamic ways, occurs precisely between the various parts of the personality. It hinders and makes it more difficult for a traumatised person to realise the traumatising experiences, but, on the other hand, it improves the patient's capacity to act when the circumstances are not favourable for forming a more integrated life story.

THE CURRENT SITUATION AND THE SPIRIT OF THE TIME

As recently as the 1980s, journalism in Finland was fettered by self-censorship as a result of having a certain great and powerful neighbour. In the past two decades I have looked at things primarily from the point of view of emotional trauma, and it seems that the social atmosphere and the possibilities for discussion have improved and become substantially freer in Finland. In 2016, Finland was chosen for the sixth time in a row as the country with the highest level of freedom of the press. The walls that hinder associative thinking – the Berlin Walls of the mind – have gradually been taken down.

Public discussion in Finland increasingly contains articles and books related to emotional trauma. The theme has become part of publicly expressed reality, social life and debate. This is a great, permanent change that has possibly even gathered momentum in the past few years. The trend has already had an influence on many disciplines, but the field of psychiatry, and maybe medicine more generally, seems to be somewhat conservative in this respect.

Contemporary psychiatry tries to reduce a range of things to one level of reality: brain chemistry. Psychopharmaceuticals that work on the level of receptors largely dominate treatment practices in psychiatry, even shaping our understanding of what mental disorders are. In this situation, it is healthy to hear whole stories coloured by emotional trau-matisation, as shocking and grim as they may be. The brave women who have contributed to our book are determined to write and share their stories, despite all the disappointments and failed meetings they have experienced during their journeys – which is a good thing, as it is easier for people to identify with human beings and their life stories than with neurotransmitters in the brain.

Trauma is a good starting-point for future psychiatry in that, un-like present trends in psychiatry, it can make extensive use of theoret-ical frames of reference. Theories create a new type of psychobiologi-cal foundation, enabling us to understand and study severe psychiatric disorders through biology, using evolutionary concepts. This makes the whole discipline more valid, vigorous and logical. Trauma theories (Van der Hart et al., 2006) and theories on the autonomic nervous system (Porges, 2011), affective neuroscience (Panksepp, 1998), consciousness (Edelman & Tononi, 2000) and the organism–environment relationship (Järvilehto, 1994; Rayner & Järvilehto, 2008) can all be integrated into a coherent view – a view that really helps people recover from trauma-re-lated mental disorders: that is, from all dissociative disorders.

In addition, the recent, highly praised approaches of epigenetics and neuroflexibility (plasticity) can be applied to and seamlessly united with the framework of emotional traumatisation. Epigenetics focuses on the continuous interaction of genes and environmental impacts. In this in-teraction, the activation and extinction of genes are actually controlled by what happens in the environment: that is, by the experiences one has in life. It is no longer possible to distinguish between the impact of genes and the impact of the environment. Plasticity, in turn, refers to the fact that the central nervous system is the part of a human being that can change the most, and we can, for good reason, say that the same applies to the control of the autonomic nervous system. Plasticity is at its high-est in childhood (Diseth, 2005).

I see the so-called positivistic ethos of science, which still continues to influence all of society, as being especially ill-suited for psychiatry. Something essential is lost in this tradition of science from which "all meaning has been stripped" (positivism). Taking a positivistic approach makes it impossible to see the connection between the life story and the mental health or condition of a person. Sacrificed on the altar of objectivity and declared value-free, scientific psychiatry becomes a mechanical, fragmented discipline with no history. It becomes estranged from its actual purpose – healing – and is instead satisfied with alleviating and turning off symptoms through long-term medication.

The use of a trauma-oriented frame of reference also implies that old-fashioned Cartesianism, the stark separation of mind and body, is drawing its last breaths before expiring. The new approach enables us to pursue a more practice-oriented development of science. Additionally, technology has opened up new possibilities especially through imaging. Instead of just mapping symptoms in order to provide medication, we can move on to understanding wholes and witnessing a new surge of narrativity – perhaps gradually in scientific psychiatry as well. Through the perspective of traumatisation, symptoms acquire real meaning. They can reveal important phases in the patient's life. Symptoms will build up logical wholes, which will make working with mental health challenging, interesting and effective in a new way. Psychiatry is becoming meaningful.

Perhaps at some point, the scientific community will be brave enough to acknowledge that psychiatric diagnostics based only on describing symptoms is not valid. Certainly, there are still many problems on the way. Big ships turn slowly.

THE TRAUMA BECOMES VISIBLE

One no longer needs to be ashamed of and silent about traumas. Their existence cannot be denied socially and collectively any longer. By now, a majority of people understand that there are pressing problems in our society. The grassroots level that we authors represent is crucial in making change possible. In Finland, the change is irreversible, as an increasing number of "precedents" are appearing in various contexts.

War traumas may now, with new generations, be so distant in Finland that their impact no longer hinders more elaborate reflection on painful issues. Socially, subcultures have become more diverse and fragmented, which has also contributed to an atmosphere in which things can be discussed more freely. We may also call this change a post-modern trend in which all flowers are allowed to bloom more freely – something that is possible especially in Finland, the model country for freedom of speech. This development has, in its most recent phase, been shaped and sped up by a dramatic cultural-anthropological change in the digital world: social media.

A fairly high level of gender equality has doubtless, in many ways, been achieved in Finland. Finnish women were the first women to be enfranchised in Europe and to become eligible – to stand as candidates in elections – in the whole world. Still, the situation is not so simple. In its editorial on Women's Day 2017, the biggest Finnish newspaper, Helsingin Sanomat, stated that despite the fact that Finland is actively working to improve the position of women and girls internationally, we have the dubious honour of being the second most violent country for women in the European Union.

For some time I have been reflecting on to what extent different forms of subjugation cause mental disorders. The answer is probably to a great extent. There is a tendency to support a scientific view which "externalises" responsibility, placing it on genes. However, the polyvagal theory on the autonomic nervous system (cf. Porges, 2011) brings a whole new perspective to the issues of subjugation and submission, scientifically spotlighting human interaction in an interesting way.

It is extremely difficult to grasp and, for many stakeholders, very painful to admit that there may be fundamental flaws in the structures and activities of the treatment system itself that can be described by the concept of "power asymmetry". United Nations Special Rapporteur Professor Dainius Pūras has mentioned power asymmetries as one of the three major obstacles that either hamper or even prevent real advances in psychiatry. Such a distortion and asymmetry in structural power create an environment in which human rights violations can also take place. It is one of the key factors perpetuating the unsatisfactory state in which psychiatry is today, the status quo of psychiatry (cf. Pūras, 2017). This offers us an important view into how treatment can, in addition to being ineffective, also traumatise patients anew.

Award-winning non-fiction and fiction literature in Finland has lately provided us with precise descriptions that have traumatisation as their common denominator. Recently, Ville Kivimäki's *Murtuneet mielet* ("Broken Minds") won the Finlandia Prize for Non-Fiction, and *Kangastus 38* ("Mirage 38") by Kjell Westö was awarded the Nordic Literature Prize. Both books were published in 2013 and contain powerful accounts of how the structural dissociation of the personality is manifested.

Trauma-oriented psychotherapy has guidelines and features that are surprisingly similar to those involved in peace negotiations between countries – something Finns are good at. In both processes, cooperation between different parties must be created, possibilities and conditions for negotiations need to be found, and the sense of security must be increased by taking various views into consideration in a balanced way (Haavisto, 2011). It would be nice to see this approach and strategy applied more often both in contemporary politics and in the sphere of science so that we could see real communication. That would allow us to sit down at the negotiation table. When doing research on something as complex as emotional traumatisation, progress requires real interaction and cooperation. This also applies to circumstances involving different disciplines. Emotional traumatisation does not concern only psychiatry: it is important for society in general. Research on trauma requires cooperation between different fields: that is, a cross- or multi-disciplinary approach.

A fine example of this kind of multi-disciplinary approach is the doctoral thesis of Päivi Rissanen, who has, in an interesting way, examined and related her personal experience of psychiatric treatment from the point of view of social policy by applying methods used in the humanities (Rissanen, 2015). In the field of social policy – in the Faculty of Social Sciences – it has been possible to do such a study. In different fields, research cultures can develop in different directions. Rissanen's thesis bravely opens up doors of possibilities and is, thus, also invaluable for society.

A clear sign of a cultural change on the international level is the responsible attitude that the Catholic Church and the present pope have assumed concerning the mistreatment of children within the Church. Strikingly, this problem is connected with a dominant religion, as the Catholic Church is the biggest Christian church in the world. Thus, we are not talking about a sect or a marginal problem, but a mainstream issue: something that threatens the majority of Christians. What the Church earlier concealed and kept silent about, it now acknowledges and takes responsibility for. In addition to apologising, the Church has paid billions of euros in damages on both sides of the Atlantic. We can speculate to what extent these problems led to the surprising, premature resignation of the previous pope – a decision that is almost unheard of. In 2016, the Academy Award for Best Picture was awarded to Spotlight, which tells about the gradual disclosure of the tragedy of child abuse within the Catholic Church.

It is perfectly clear that even dealing with trauma-related issues and the promotion of a new way of thinking will arouse and meet intense and diverse opposition. We often run into the same phenomenon on a smaller scale in families in which severe childhood traumatisation has occurred. The comprehensive, analytical and narrative information on traumatisation in this book is not based on expressions of horror, juxtaposition or the desire to expose scandals: the stories deal with and tell about things calmly, critically and profoundly. That is the best way of searching for the truth. The same applies to psychotherapy that seeks to heal patients with trauma-related disorders.

Looking at the present trend, we can expect that an increasing number of stories dealing with a variety of childhood traumas will be published and read. It is important to hear accounts of encouraging healing processes, because nothing will probably be as effective as such accounts in breaking the collective wall of denial; gradually, they will give birth to a broader consciousness. I know many people who plan, within a few years, to write about how they have recovered from their childhood traumas. I myself will not do this until after my working career has ended, as now it is time for me to focus on other tasks that will improve the situation of traumatised people. This book is, as such, a precedent that shows the way.

This book will strengthen a change in psychiatry at a time when the subject of traumatisation is advancing, springing up in many contexts and spheres of society. The era of silence will gradually be brought to an end.

A Matter of Life and Death

The Power of Nature

REALISATION

From the point of view of healthy development and the capacity to function, it is useful for all people – and even nations – to understand their past, as today's actions and choices are essentially based on history and earlier experiences. Thus, it is essential never to stop learning and growing as a human being. Have we learned the lessons of the past?

Realisation means that experiences and their personal meaning have been understood and integrated into a wider whole, a life story. The more one's experiences deviate from that which is considered ordinary, from prevailing socially determined norms and the surrounding culture, the more difficult it is to realise one's traumatic experiences, to reconcile them within one's personality. Crucially, realisation requires that one can express experiences verbally, so that they can be understood, and safely shared, by another person. Pierre Janet understood how important and central it is for us as human beings to tell stories. Unfortunately, he was forgotten in dynamic psychiatry for almost a century while Sigmund Freud dominated the field (cf. Ellenberger, 1970).

For every human being, the most efficient way of attaining realisation is discussion: that is, offering one's experiences to another person so that these experiences can be examined and assessed critically but with empathy. The truth heals, no matter what it looks like. Naturally, the pace at which one can face the truth depends very much on the individual. One's success in facing the truth depends on the circumstances at a given point, one's ability to regulate feelings and, above all, the available external support.

There are always limits to how well we can integrate our experiences and grasp their meanings, as we are always imperfect, human. The more painful and out of line one's experiences are, the harder it is to integrate them. In addition to resilience, an advanced sense of proportion is one of the most important pre-conditions for trauma treatment. To facilitate recovery from traumas, Janet developed a psychology of action which can be applied to all people.

For traumatised people, facing the past is more difficult, but in a special way because of the structure of the personality. This structure is rather commonly misunderstood in the field of psychiatry in Finland. Often, professionals do not even suspect dissociation. And the consequences are grave. The problem is systematic and partly a result of the prevailing diagnostics of psychiatry and the way it guides observations. It is also caused by the fact that trauma tends to be hidden; this hiding occurs in diverse ways, with the aim of allowing a person to go on living and be accepted in his or her social environment.

The present description-based diagnostics focuses too much on individual symptoms; therefore, it cannot see wider meaningful wholes. Furthermore, this system of diagnostics generally discards aetiological assumptions: it does not focus on the causes of illness. Often, its starting-point is on the level of cerebral neurotransmitters rather than the level of telling stories. This promotes and maintains collective denial: that is, a narrative and an illusion of a society in which people, especially children, are not mistreated and traumatised emotionally. Or a society in which damaging experiences are not connected with mental disorders. This denial hinders the process of realisation which is necessary for real healing.

According to the general principles of neuroplasticity, the development of a child's personality is affected above all by his or her environment and social interactions. We cannot be held responsible for the environment, family or community into which we are born. Special professional competence, knowledge and skill are needed so that a person's life story can be rebuilt safely and persistently, jointly and in cooperation; then, it is possible to share and realise even the experience that Janet described as "the action of triumph". Eventually, such experiences will lead to a situation in which structural dissociation will gradually become unnecessary. In a successful therapeutic process, symptoms are reduced as a kind of spin-off effect.

I am delighted every time I hear that my patients consider me a safe person. This is an important response, because there can be no growth of realisation without a sense of security – a sense that can be achieved through repeated and long-term successful situations of interaction. We all do our best when we feel secure. As a therapist, I naturally have to consider the sense of security constantly and take various corrective actions in order to improve and restore it. This is extremely educational and makes one humble. The interactive regulation of emotions is one of the most important spheres in which therapists can improve themselves. It also seems essential that the therapist is open to learning new things and able to feel genuine delight in discovery, as a therapist who is set in his or her ways may not feel safe enough for the patient.

When suffering is shared successfully, it is not in vain. Because sharing heals.

TRUSTING THE PERSON

Considering how important it is to achieve the capacity for realisation, it is very harmful not to believe what people tell you. It becomes especially problematic if those providing treatment base their work on immediately questioning what their patient tells them – whatever the reason might be. Whether because of the Finnish mentality or our culture, not once in my career have I met a patient who tried to imitate a DID patient: that is, a patient who attempted to gain secondary benefits (for example, getting attention) by pretending to have this mental disorder. As a matter of fact, I have been astonished at the extent to which such possible cases of fraud have, in other countries, been considered a substantial problem that needs to be addressed. Think of the harm that is done to healing at the very beginning of treatment if the professional starts the process by doubting the authenticity of the patient's experiences!

Instead, I frequently run into situations in my work in which the system of treatment has not been able, at any point, to notice, verbalise or meet the dissociative psychopathology with therapeutic precision. Actually, the structure of the patient's personality often becomes evident only in a relationship based on long-term treatment. However, unfortunately our treatment system does not appreciate such relationships enough.

It is naive to think that everything a patient – or anyone – says is simply true. Naivety is a sign of a considerable lack of self-criticism.

However, it is equally narrow-minded not to connect the story of the patient with a broader view: the totality of the behaviour, symptoms and non-verbal communication in particular. What matters is not only what is said: the way of saying it and what is left unsaid also matter. A professional who is armed with and steadfastly trusts in questionnaires cannot necessarily pay attention to non-verbal or indirect communication nor, above all, analyse the whole picture. Partly, the problem rises when a professional considers that arriving at a diagnosis at the beginning of treatment is so important that he or she may, for the sake of diagnosis, sacrifice even the creation of a good, trustful relationship with the patient. The situation is also problematic if the diagnosis is given from above with no explanations or discussion, with no cooperation with the patient.

My opinion is that having a diagnosis is not of primary importance in treatment. As my approach applies the principles of Janet's psychology of action, diagnostic issues do not interfere with the creation of a treatment relationship. The aim is to produce corrective experiences from the first meetings on. At the same time, successful meetings also serve the purpose of diagnosis. If the patient finally feels that he or she is being seen profoundly, we may witness the rise of a positive vortex between a new kind of understanding and experiences of security.

Broadly speaking, we are dealing with trust, the crucial foundation on which all secure and healing psychotherapy is based. Trust is a process which, in principle, is assessed continuously. When there is a great deal of trust, big, positive things can happen.

THE PURPOSE OF THE BOOK

I am simply delighted about this book. It enables all those who are interested in the subject of dissociative disorders to read stories that have not been told earlier though attempts have been made to tell them both with and without words. I have respect and empathy for all the suffering expressed in these life stories. I am deeply proud of the courage the other authors show in telling about their lives. Putting one's experiences in an autobiographical, verbal form is both a sign of considerable progress in the therapeutic process and, at the same time, healing. It is extremely beneficial to the process of integration to tell your story verbally and through images and videos instead of just through behaviour or "inexplicable symptoms".

I believe that this book can open up a new perspective into the world of trauma for the reader. It will complement earlier evidence on the special features of trauma and structural dissociation. It will provide validation for us who have been traumatised: we do exist.

I am confident that this book will give strength to many people who have been isolated, silenced or ignored despite their difficulties; it will enable them to trust that their stories are important and can be told in a secure setting, and that these stories contain a great deal of truth and, above all, the keys to healing.

The ability to see the overall picture, a questioning attitude, and connecting and realising both past and present scenes are all an important part of our mental health. The same applies to the skill of distinguishing the past from the present and the essential from the unessential. When a moment of meeting occurs, it also repairs damage caused by shame – the feeling of not being good enough. According to my teacher, Professor Onno van der Hart, shame is frequently central in childhood traumas, though it can also be hidden. Reading about the experiences of peers is often an effective way of reducing the shame traumatised people feel.

High-quality professional literature on the treatment of traumatisation abounds in Finnish as well as in other languages, but hardly any life stories have been told by traumatised people themselves. This book fills this gap in a fine way. Five Survivors, a Hundred Lives brings hope and a new level to the collective awareness that vast obstacles can be overcome. The book offers the possibility of identification to many people, especially patients suffering from complex traumatisation. At the same time, it will give an increasing number of new people the courage to tell their stories and break the silence. Real-life stories that create hope may be the most natural way of conveying information and promoting understanding.

The stories in our book show beautifully what an enormous capacity waits to be set free in the world of severe psychological disorders and in people who are used to coping in extreme circumstances. It will come forth if these people can be met in the right way: humanely and with an approving attitude. This book is just the tip of an iceberg.

It is likely that extremely grave experiences of traumatisation will not be received collectively until the possibility of healing – at least partial repair of the damage – is available. It is also easier to diagnose a disorder if there is an effective and convincing cure. For example, the discovery of medical treatment has obviously had a substantial impact on even the development of disorder classification in the history of psychiatry. To benefit from increased healing, professionals and treatment systems need to acknowledge many harsh facts. It may prove to be impossible to do this if there is no hope. The primary purpose of our book is to give hope, both to people who are traumatised and to those who are trying to understand, help and cure them.

Pierre Janet, the most important pioneer of trauma treatment, made better treatment of mental problems available as early as the 1800s (see, e.g., Van der Hart et al., 2006; Ogden et al., 2006). At the time, the social atmosphere was not yet ready to receive his valuable theories. Are we ready to receive them today?

At best, our book may even inspire scientific psychiatry to change its course. There is a need to take development at grassroots level into consideration and do some reassessment. It is time to face and actively focus on trauma-related psychological disorders. We can certainly no longer be ignored –thanks in part to the Internet.

GRATITUDE

How relieved and grateful I feel to have a chance to cooperate, share, work and be part of healing processes! For this sense of fulfilment, I am deeply grateful to all my patients and colleagues: that is, my peers and the variety of shared journeys.

Many wise people have been clearing the way to revive and enhance Pierre Janet's legacy. Without their efforts, I would not have been able to recover from my own traumas. It gives me a feeling of security to know that so many people care for us who have been traumatised. I know that I am very fortunate in many ways; for example, I've been able to experience how a private, endless grimness and inability turns into something that is collectively good and can be shared with other people. I realise that I was extremely lucky to meet the right people at the right time. I also deeply realise that many people are not so lucky. We can and will do much for them.

These life stories in our book are invaluable in their own right, but they are also a significant part of the process of change. Sharing stories creates a new kind of peer support and sense of belonging, tribalisation – something that is so important for us gregarious animals called humans. Real cooperation requires meeting. Empathetic, respectful moments of meeting between people also work as a model for cooperation between the different parts of a person's personality. This book is a sign of a new type of cooperation and can serve as an example for any community or form of collaboration.

I am grateful to my peers for giving me the opportunity to provide my views as a mental health professional in this outstanding work.

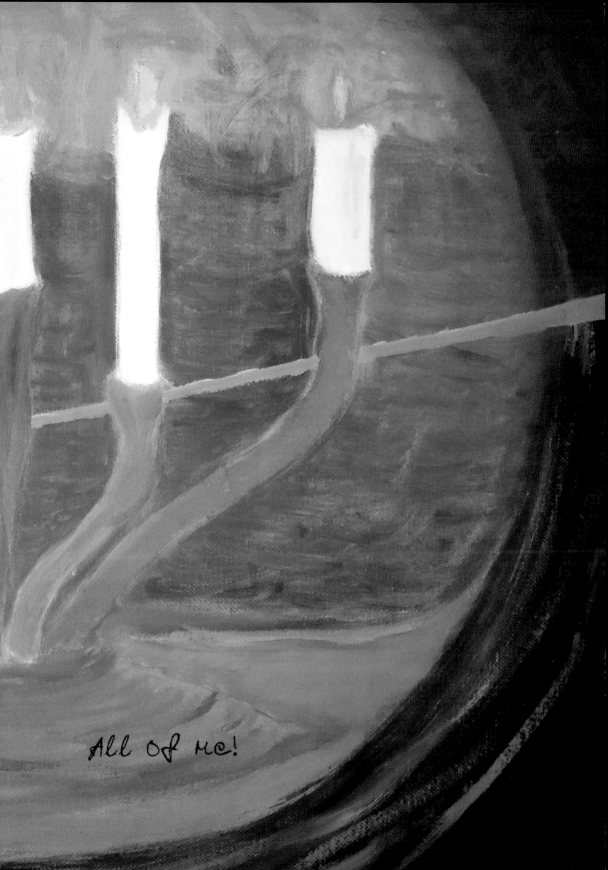

Kaisa

I'm Kaisa, a 34-year-old language teacher. Nowadays, my life looks quite normal.

You could be my colleague or next-door neighbour, and you'd never guess that I have a dissociative identity disorder. I'm funny and cheerful, energetic and extroverted, athletic and attractive; I'm a nice, ordinary Finnish woman. The kind who gets a bank loan and collects bonuses for her grocery shopping, who makes up her eyes in the morning and reads the local paper. A woman who has a whole other world, a hell and a heaven, inside her, but that's a secret. I have many secrets, and I've learned to carry them silently, with a nice smile on my face.

A BROKEN CHILD

When God threw me into the world from His great heavenly infant ward almost thirty-five years ago, I fell into the countryside, landing in a family that already had a rather big flock of children. At best, my childhood was characterised by quietness and modesty, by the mentality of the backwoods. We were nobody, and we had no need to become anybody. We had our sheep and cows and pigs, our hay fields, tractors and lakes, the neighbour's kids, and the milk cans. That felt safe. What didn't feel safe was that, behind the cloud, there was a huge, angry God watching everything, waiting all the time for a chance to throw a pitchfork at a mischievous or fallen child of His. My family belonged to a shitty religious community that was always right and set limits for us that were not to be crossed even with the tip of a Chinese shoe. I may have understood something wrong (or right?) already as a small child, but the community definitely didn't give me security. It offered me the fear of Doomsday, making my life hell.

I don't remember how old I was when I was sexually abused for the first time in the community, but the nice, pretty angel girl I had originally been was dead by the time I turned nine. I was a strange, delusional child, whose cries for help were not heard; I was left alone in bloody darkness. For some reason, my family and the other members of the congregation were not, at the time, able to see the horrible things that were going on. I wasn't the only one in the community who was being abused, and I now think that we children reacted so strongly that someone should have paid attention. Or maybe it just has to do with growing up: you no longer see the world as it is – you see it as you think it is and want it to be. "All the members of our congregation are God's sacred people, so something like this cannot happen in our congregation." Denial mechanisms can be strong in this kind of situations.

I suppose dissociation may also be a kind of denial mechanism. For me, the only way to cope with the violence I went through was to convince myself: This is not happening, this is not real. I remember watching what was going on from somewhere high above, near the ceiling or from the sky. Angel girls simply can't take something like that; it's better

For me, the only way to cope with the violence I went through was to convince myself: This is not happening, this is not real. I remember watching what was going on from somewhere high above, near the ceiling or from the sky. Angel girls simply can't take something like that; it's better for them to fly to Jesus or beyond consciousness for them to fly to Jesus or beyond consciousness. I wanted to be light, lighter. The night sky was gradually lit by my lightness; it radiated freedom, the sweet bliss of flight, emptiness, nonexistence. In daily reality, I quit eating; I lost so much weight that I hardly existed. This attracted the attention of the school nurse, but eventually I slipped through all the support systems and safety nets. Nothing prevented me from going crazy. I was a violent child who was self-destructive in every way possible.

At the age of ten, my situation got a bit better for two reasons. Firstly, certain coincidental practical things meant that the physical sexual abuse came to an end, at least for me. Secondly, my mind closed up and twisted; it was nicely dislocated. I was no longer actively aware of or recalled most of the things I'd gone through. As far as I understand, the onset of dissociation was, in my case, connected with conscious and voluntary as well as unconscious detachment and denial. The world was unbearable, so I had to make it bearable with the help of my mind. I stared at the ceiling, kept opening and closing my eyes, slid away. I split my mind first once and then once more. I told myself: This is not happening, this doesn't exist, and it stopped happening, stopped existing. If you can't bear the life you have been given, you must make a new and better one for yourself.

Then I got a best friend, a boy who was a year older than me. His name was Joel, and he made my life bearable again. I could talk about anything to Joel: he listened to me and understood. The only special thing about this was that Joel only existed for me: he lived and resided only in my head, in my broken soul and heart. Instead of being one, I had become two: Kaisa-Joel, Joel-Kaisa. At some point, I realised that it was dangerous to talk about Joel to other people, and I gradually learned to take control of my crazy world. I watched how my classmates behaved and read books: this is the way to behave, be, talk. A normal person will talk like this and act like this, while these kinds of behaviour will raise eyebrows. I had no inner code or sense of how people should behave, but I was a clever girl and got only A's at school, so I managed to figure out how to cope in daily life.

Nevertheless, I didn't consider the inner reality of my head as normal nor myself as "an average person": I always just pretended to be normal. I heard the term "dissociation" for the first time only in 2012. Thus, for decades, I didn't have a name for my way of being, but I realised that I was different and tried to hide myself. And I was fairly successful in doing so until I turned twenty-one.

All of these vintage images used in Kaisas story are from her old childhood scrapbooks

A DESPERATE ADOLESCENT

In my teens, everything still ran fairly normally. I had an eating disorder, and, in my own secret darkness, I was grimly self-destructive. I cut myself and wished I could die, which I actually didn't think of as anything uniquely strange or alarming. I guess I thought that the kind of devilish horrors I had in my dreams were also part of other people's dreams. My inner world became increasingly diverse instead of growing integrated. The bullying I went through at school gave birth to new, aggressive personality parts in me. I wasn't aware of all my childhood traumas, though my body bore marks of them. I carried the stigma of a whore in me, because sexual abuse had caused severe physical damage to me. I've never sought help for the injuries, but they've certainly hindered me from having the normal life of an adult woman.

What I've said here may seem in contradiction to the appearance of my life. In adolescence, I had many friends and was engaged in both physical activities and art; I was still the best pupil in my class. At some point, I realised I was sexually interested in a girl in my class. A toss of her hair, an inviting smile – and I was lost. But the thought of being a lesbian was unbearable: now I'd end up in hell for sure, and if my family found out, I'd be thrown out of the house, into the snow. To hide my perverted nature, I got a boyfriend. Going out with him was definitely a cover operation at first, but with time I fell in love and became attached to this person who always treated me well. We got married years later, and our marriage lasted over ten years; no doubt, it was the most coherent, stable and healthy time of my life, maybe even something exceptional for a dissociative person. We had a good life. I didn't think of my husband primarily as a man, because I had trouble with the thought, but he was a dear, trustworthy companion who filled my days with light.

I finished secondary school with good grades, and the summer after I graduated I was admitted to university to study exactly what I wanted. However, I didn't study long before I became tired. Normal life demanded too much of me; I had exhausted my resources. The contradiction between my inner world and the exterior world was too great. What was real? Did I even exist? Without thinking too much – spontaneously and almost as clinically as a psychopath – I tried to commit suicide. The attempt was a shock but also a total surprise for everyone who knew me, as I was the opposite of a problem youth: Miss My-Perfect-Life-Smiles.

Via a somatic ward, I ended up on a psychiatric ward – in the middle of the chemical revolution of the late 1990s. I talked about the voices in my head and climbed the walls; I tried to harm myself again and again. The closed doors made me feel anxious, and I felt that life was a never-ending line of hells and prisons. But the worst locks were in my head, as I couldn't escape myself and my memories. The burning firestorm of agony in me made it impossible to breathe. I didn't want to go on; I was like an animal facing the hunter's gun, cornered and exhausted. I was just praying for the mercy shot.

I was diagnosed as schizophrenic and given some twenty antipsychotic pills to take every day. I slept eighteen hours a day, put on eighty kilos and became apathetic. A year went by, then another, and a third one. The world glided by me. I didn't feel well, but the diagnosis was also a relief. After all, I was neither the Devil's daughter nor God's bride. I was ill.

I spent years on a closed ward. The health care officials declared me unable to work. I talked about my traumas, but wasn't given any psychotherapy. At times, the doctors disagreed about my diagnosis, and my medication was adjusted hundreds of times. Nothing helped: despair wouldn't loosen its grip on me.

I tried to commit suicide numerous times, and almost succeeded. One of the attempts left me with a heart defect. Your relationship to death changes when you've looked it in the eye. Once you've settled the score with it, it's no longer so frightening, which is unfortunate. Your relationship to suicide is also changed. To turn against yourself requires that you extinguish the ultimate instinct in yourself: the instinct for self-protection. This cannot be done without a certain level of madness. Despite the fact that you own your self and your life, the title to it expires when you turn your hand against life. Suicide must be prevented, always. Life is incredibly, immensely valuable, and unique.

Indeed, I'm not the only dissociative patient who has ended up with the label schizophrenic. I've felt bitter about the lost years, but if I let

bitterness overtake me, there would be no end to it – after everything I've gone through. Shit happens, and then you move on. Nevertheless, the years spent in hospital have changed me in a way. I've witnessed so many different life stories that I'll always feel empathy for the weak. Siberia teaches you a lesson; Siberia makes you more of a leftist.

I was saved by the fact that I got so physically ill from antipsychotics that I had to stop taking them. To the doctors' surprise and even irritation, I got much better. I began to hear my own voice. The medicine had taken away even my last sense of reality, but now my physical stupor vanished and I felt that I was alive again, at least to some extent. I lost weight and my body recovered in other respects, too. I returned to my studies, met a doctor who identified and recognised the dissociative disorder, and I was sent to therapy.

A CONFUSED ADULT

I'm still not whole. Dissociation manifests itself in me in many ways; for example, it's difficult for me to have normal feelings. I may be quite cheerful at the funeral of someone who's dear to me and in agony when I face happiness. Mostly, I'm relatively emotionless, but I don't treat other people coldly. I have fairly healthy morals, and I'm capable of love and altruism. I suppose I'm emotionless only with respect to myself and my memories. It would be impossible to live in society if I recognised the hell of my childhood, so I distance it from myself. Unfortunately, this means that I don't know myself at all – no matter what kind of successful career or normal life I might have ahead of me. To quote the Finnish poet Uuno Kailas: The me in me is being dragged around by someone I do not know.

My personality is clearly split so that my student friends from the university, for example, notice the

64

difference when they meet me in leisure time: my student self is much more efficient, open and relaxed than my reserved self at home. I'm least aware of my past in the world of study. I can't feel anything; nothing touches me. My memory works in a completely different way than in leisure time: I never forget the smallest detail. I don't like to bring anything connected with my studies home; it just doesn't work.

I'm socially and verbally talented, and I get along with people. I make friends easily, and I'm not afraid of giving speeches and getting up in front of people. Nevertheless, social situations are tiring for me, as I sense and feel other people's emotions too intensely. I try to adjust and conform to people's expectations. I can see from their reactions how I should behave. Sometimes it's difficult for me to bear the flood of feelings and thoughts rolling over me. I can't keep my boundaries safe. I may be almost unable to function when leaving the hairdresser, for example. I don't know where I am or where I'm going. The social situation has exhausted me, because the hairdresser's conscious and unconscious emotional messages and signals have penetrated my defences.

PROBLEMS WITH MEMORY

Dissociation is also about both remembering and forgetting. For me, the disorder causes two kinds of memory blocks. First, there's the frustrating, never-ending forgetfulness: the keys are lost, my wallet is at home, I missed the meeting. I believe this is a result of my never being really present anywhere. In my head, I'm engaged in a dialogue with Joel or the other parts of my personality, listening to echoes from the past. The voices don't come from outside my head, and I know that Joel is not "real". As far as I understand, I haven't had actual hallucinations since I was a child. Yet I don't really feel that I'm part of my environment or life, and I'm always at least partly absent, no matter what I'm doing. Thus, you could say I'm absent-minded, though I do manage to function at the level required by the challenges of daily life. Furthermore, I have no problems with my memory in the sphere of studies. According to intelligence tests, my working memory is above normal.

I also have other types of memory problems than forgetfulness in daily life. They're more complete and more difficult: at worst, I can be totally absent from my self for days at a time. When I feel threatened or become too absorbed in my memories, I can regress to the level of a child – I have no other name for this phenomenon than regression. My heart stops beating, the noise in my mind grows unbearable, I'm enveloped in a kind of mist and dream and, finally, oblivion. I scream, shriek, kick, hit, scratch, fight for my life – or I lie quiet and resigned, ready to take the pain. I don't remember these scenes at all afterwards, but other people tell me about them. Every now and then I get stuck in this condition. Sometimes, I may behave like a happy little girl, playing and singing. Fortunately, these complete lapses into the past are fairly rare these days.

It meant a great deal for me to find out that there's something called dissociative disorder. I never really believed in my schizophrenia diagnosis, and it made me feel dishonest and phony in a way. When you have a dissociative disorder you might rage and smash up the mental health office and then go and calmly give a sensible speech in a seminar at the university. It's good to know that you're not a pretender but just repeating a pattern you learned as a child. Life must go on no matter what kind of horrors took place the night before.

Recently, so-called false memories have been discussed in the media. Behind this talk lies the belief that it's possible, in principle, to implant almost any kind of idea in a human brain. Not all our memories are real. It has been claimed that therapists can even come up with traumas for their patients that they then start to believe are real.

Without committing myself to whether the theory on false memories is true or not, I want to stress that we're really in dangerous waters if therapists and doctors base their work on the premise that their clients' traumatic memories are fictitious. Getting help in Finland is difficult, almost impossible even – as I know from experience. I had to fight for fifteen years to get help for my traumas. My traumatic memories were definitely not implanted in my mind by someone else. Besides, we underestimate the professionalism of therapists if we think that they want to invent horror stories about their client's life. If this were the case, it would be a matter of much more than just false memories. Untrained therapists can, in general, harm their clients in many ways. I recommend that traumatised people in Finland use only trauma therapists recognised by the Social Services Office. It's impossible to learn professional methods in one weekend course.

No communication between people can be based on the assumption that one of the parties is lying and fabricating things. Doctors and therapists must base their work on the premise that the client is speaking the truth. A professional will not provoke memories or enjoy hearing sensational stories. He or she will let memories resurface on their own, if they will.

Whether we like it or not, awful things are done to children in Finland. If the deeds are too awful, the mind shuts the scenes off. They're unbearable, so they're removed from daily consciousness. But the scenes leave their mark, and I don't believe that any woman who's been a victim of childhood sexual abuse, for example, can lead a completely normal life until the traumas suddenly resurface in middle age. There are almost always some symptoms: self-injury, eating disorders, abuse of intoxicants, etc. The traumatised people may not even know themselves what exactly is wrong with them. They're just not well. There's a black, nameless cloud inside the head. Dissociation is a way of ensuring that life will continue, whereas being completely present mentally in a traumatic situation wouldn't allow it.

For me, the discussion on whether the existence of dissociation is recognised or not means a new approach to humanity. As recently as 10–20 years ago, the common view was that all mental disorders and diseases could be treated with the proper medication. Our thoughts, feelings, fears and traumas were explained in terms of brain chemistry. Not until recently have people begun to view things in a new context and look at a person's mental wellbeing and not-wellbeing in the same context as his or her past.

I don't believe in dwelling on things. Wallowing in your traumas serves no purpose: if there's a fire, you must get out. However, if the development of your self and your identity has been hindered or gone astray because of certain conditions, you won't be able to lead a normal life until the situation has been corrected. I've also started to feel the need to talk about the past. That's just the way the mind works. I can no longer carry this burden alone and guard the secrets. Fortunately, my therapist is a professional who doesn't pull anything out of me by force. If I want to let her in on my traumas, she will listen and help me cope with them.

DAILY LIFE: A CHALLENGE

I try to keep my daily life as regular and stress-free as possible and avoid talking too much about my traumas. A steady rhythm of life with no surprises is good for me. However, I can stand a great deal of work-related stress and actually like it when stress at work or in my studies prevents me from thinking too much. I'm also active in sports, as it gives me a sense of being in the here and now.

My husband had it rough by my side. Luckily, he learned to recognise my symptoms well and often managed to return me to the present. Still, there were times when I couldn't recognise even him in my agony; it was sad. Dissociation was in the end one of the reasons for our divorce. It's difficult to live with a traumatised person. I'm grateful to my ex-husband, and we're still good friends. There's a new love in my life, and my partner in this relationship also has a traumatic background. The good thing about this is that a personal experience of dissociation helps one understand one's partner. On the other hand, two extremely broken people wouldn't be able to mend each other. I need a great deal of security and regularity in my life because of my dissociative disorder and traumas.

In terms of therapy, I've come quite far. Interestingly, the process of integration is also connected with something uncomfortable: as my life increasingly becomes my own, my sad memories may push their way even into my world at the university. I'm more and more aware of my whole self and my past. Dissociation retreats, which is not just a relief, because I have to be able to bear my trauma without the protection of lack of feeling and recollection. This is hard and requires tools offered by therapy.

All my life, I've been troubled by the feeling that I don't exist. Often I even keep repeating my own confusion loudly: I don't exist. Not here. Nowhere. This isn't real. I'm not real. Paradoxically, I also experience strongly that I'm many people, not just one. My personality is not coherent, and neither is my life history. For example, when I read my case records I feel extremely disoriented: who are these reports talking about?

My world-view is equally confused. It's difficult for me to grasp what's real and what's imaginary, and I can, for example, forget that The Lord of the Rings is just a story. In my teens, I imagined I knew the Finnish poet Saima Harmaja, and, as a child, I thought I saw angels. I absorb myself so completely in the world of books and films that I have a hard time returning to daily life. I seldom feel that the world around me is real. To be sure, I need to regularly listen to the sounds of my environment or touch the arm of the person I'm talking to.

I can understand why my experience of the world is so weak. I lived my childhood in hell, in a world that shouldn't be anyone's reality. Still, people around me, like my schoolmates and their parents, led perfectly normal lives – usually without noticing anything strange about me. Nothing made sense, as the hell and my daily reality couldn't be united. The same sense of unreality still follows me. What's real?

On the other hand, I'm highly rational in daily life. The adult part of my personality – Kaisa – doesn't believe in fortune-tellers, meditation or spirituality. I was raised to believe in a religious world-view, but I've also had trouble swallowing its truths. I assume that if I had had a normal childhood, I'd be a completely level-headed and wholesome person, a both-feet-on-the-ground type to the hilt, who could never be drawn into building castles in the air. Dissociation is a disorder in its own right, but I'm not insane – though I am split.

From time to time, I suffer from intense physical and mental numbness. My childhood traumas taught me to shut off physical pain, too, and I can still do that. As an adult, I've had a gynaecological operation that failed and also a few other medical operations that normally would have caused almost unbearable pain; I felt nothing during them. Numbness works in smaller things, too: during blood tests, I don't feel the pricking of the needle, and I never take a local anaesthetic at the dentist's, because I don't feel any pain even when a tooth is removed. At worst, I've lost my sense of touch completely and have, for example, burnt myself by accident with an iron or hot water.

I also suffer from other sensory changes connected with dissociation: occasional colour blindness and the inability to feel fatigue, hunger, thirst and especially the cold. Such sensory aberrations make daily life more difficult, because I don't remember to eat or drink when I lose my sense of time, or I may go out in light clothes when it's freezing cold in winter. Thus, mental and physical numbness are both a good and a bad thing. In my childhood, numbness was primarily an advantage: a being that feels could never have survived rape. Now that the conditions are normal, dissociation is, in a manner of speaking, excessive combat equipment: heavy armour that you carry needlessly since the war is over.

I mostly sleep well nowadays, but I need at least half an hour to fall asleep in the evening. My inner parts have things to tell, and it takes time to listen to and calm them. Without a regular sleep rhythm, I don't have the energy to cope. When I was in hospital a few years ago, a part of my personality that wouldn't let me sleep took charge. It was convinced that something awful would happen at night, as was often the case when I was a child. I ended up being awake on the ward for more than a week, and slept badly afterwards, too. I can't understand how I survived staying awake so long. It was terrible. I thought I'd die from lack of sleep. My coordination got weaker and weaker, and it was hard for me not to fall down. I couldn't sleep though I was given prescriptions for five kinds of sleeping pills. I didn't even fall asleep though I attempted suicide by taking a huge amount of sedatives. The doctor on call was astounded: "You've taken a suicidal amount of Diapam, and yet you just sit there, staring." I only wanted to sleep; I was totally exhausted, but my child part didn't give me permission. It was too frightened. It didn't allow me to sleep even when the doctors prescribed a huge dose of Dormicum, an extremely narcotic medicine. This period was one of the roughest ones in my life. Fortunately, it's over now, but, to some extent, I still suffer from a fear of sleeping.

Thus, I don't particularly like sleeping or eating; they're just things that need to be done. I have them on my list of daily routines: after sleeping eight hours I can tick the item "sleep". I keep my daily life together with strict routines. I have orthorexia and obsessive-compulsive disorder (OCD). I control both my own and other people's doings, and I'm neurotically clean and pathologically strict when it comes to hygiene. I like lists, schedules, tasks and measurable things. I'm extremely work- and performance-oriented. Being constantly in control tires me, and I can hardly ever rest. I don't even dare to, for what might I remember and hear if I paused for a while? On the other hand, I don't consider even this extreme control of my life to be entirely bad, as it would be impossible to cope with the dissociative disorder and the various parts of my personality if my life went to pieces externally. I need clear limits and frameworks; they bring me security. I don't dare to ease up until I've got much closer to integration.

My occasional need to end up in prison or a tightly closed mental hospital has been an extreme form of my control. This is also connected with my feeling of being evil: I'm disgusting and evil, I must be put away. As a matter of fact, I've even tried to get into a psychiatric clinic so that the world would be safe from me, so that I wouldn't be able to hurt anyone. And this is really the way it works – I haven't sought isolation in order to be protected. The human mind is paradoxical: I'm even too obedient and law-abiding, and yet I feel that I'm completely worthless.

If I hadn't got into a relationship with my ex-husband when I suffered from teenage anxiety, I probably would have stayed single or begun a relationship with a woman. Our marriage turned out relatively happy, in the end. I never wanted children. I didn't feel I'd be fit to be a mother after all I'd gone through. I'm afraid of children and shun them; they're threatening to me. I don't want to have them near me.

JOEL AND THE OTHERS

My personality consists of two almost equal parts: Kaisa and Joel. My body belongs to Kaisa, a woman in her 30s. As I described earlier, I'm clearly split into a work-oriented and a leisure self even when I'm Kaisa. I guess this may not be completely exceptional, though, in my case, we're talking about a more radical switch than people's normal switches between social roles. In me, there's also Joel, a cheerful eight-year-old boy. He represents everything that's good in me. He's pure.

Boys cannot be raped.

I also recognise other inner voices in me, and their existence makes me anxious. There are homosexual parts in me. Parts with eating disorders. Aggressive, fighting, screaming parts. Small, panicking children. A ten-year-old girl who's scared. A defiant teenager who constantly has her middle finger extended. However, these other sides of my personality are not as clearly separate identities as Joel is. Rather, they're echoes from the past.

The Kaisa who runs everyday life – the adult part of my personality – usually has complete control of the different parts. It must be this way – otherwise, life would be chaos. At present, I'd never listen to my inner parts on what to wear or eat, for example. Indeed, there's so much noise always going on in my head that it's difficult for me to choose. Therefore, I like routines, rules and lists. I seldom do anything out of the ordinary. I have to cling persistently to Kaisa's lifestyle and habits. For example, I always dress in a very feminine way, since that's what I believe women do. Style isn't very important for me, and none of the parts of my personality are very fond of it, but it's part of the picture in a way. I can't always listen to the opinions of my inner voices.

But this hasn't always been the case. I remember how we practised for the matriculation exam in English at upper secondary school: Joel did the listening exam for me because I wasn't feeling well. I flunked the exam. On the psychiatric ward, I sometimes let all the parts of my personality speak at the same time. As a result, I was diagnosed with schizophrenia. Occasionally when I'm taken over by regression, I may lose my memory and find myself somewhere without remembering how I got there. Of course, this is frightening, but luckily it's rare nowadays. I may also hear from other people that what I'm saying contains contradictions or that my opinions change constantly, which makes me feel bad, since honesty is important for me. I guess I might just be disagreeing with my selves at times. There's no continuum.

My earlier diagnoses included, in addition to schizophrenia, borderline personality disorder. Indeed, I was very unstable earlier – and still am, despite my attempts to control myself and my life. I now realise that my instability is caused by my condition, in which I, with the parts of my personality switching and gliding, experience these parts' feelings, fears and often infantile solutions to problematic situations in body and soul. Though I'm a woman in my 30s who should in principle react to things like missing a bus by getting angry at worst, my self may, in such situations, be taken over by an inner panicking child, who can only respond to uncertainty by being petrified. Thus, instead of calling a taxi, I may go home to cry and sleep. My child parts are overwhelmed by the emotions of my traumatic period, and these feelings affect my adult self, too – often too strongly. A child doesn't have the same solutions and sense of proportion that an adult has.

Joel's way of speaking and handwriting differ from mine, and the same applies to his gestures and expressions. I've mainly heard about them from other people, but I can see even in a photograph whether the features belong to Joel or Kaisa. I know that we're not separate people, and yet I feel that way.

I like Joel. He's my best friend and represents all my good qualities. I'd never want to give him up, so the idea of integrating my personalities feels somewhat sad. Despite what Hollywood suggests, dissociation hardly ever means that the secret personality of a clever woman will

73

go around in the city at night, killing people with an axe. It's all about the past being in pieces inside us. I'm broken, yet the pieces are part of my life. My self is not complete because it's been crushed; nevertheless, it's mine, and it hurts to give up my pieces. As awful as being a victim of sexual abuse was, it created a very nice boy named Joel who lives and breathes inside me. Sometimes I wish the world could know him.

NO EASY MATTER: FEELINGS

My scale of feelings extends from one extreme to the other, and I've always had annoyingly few so-called normal feelings. Ninety per cent of the time I'm a machine that works, not a human being with emotions. Once, I was a sensitive child living in hell who had to numb herself in order to survive. I have a clear sense of justice and I mainly treat other people well, but mostly because I know it's correct – not because it feels right.

The lack of feelings helps me function in daily life. I don't necessarily feel disturbed even when I read in the paper about children being mistreated. When I talk about my own past, I feel as if I were telling a story or fairy-tale that has nothing to do with me. I don't feel anything, it doesn't touch me. However, there are times when my protective walls fail and a memory floods all the way to my consciousness – the part with feelings. The trigger can be a sound, a photo, a smell, a taste or the tiniest thing. My reactions to this are extreme: I yell, kick, scream, scratch, try to flee, hit myself and others, smash things. Often, I leave myself completely and my memory crumbles away. Falling into such states often happens so quickly that I have no time to stop the course of events. But now that I'm making progress in recovery, I do increasingly recognise the "tunnel conditions" that precede the attacks: that is, the moments when my senses become less acute, I get dizzy and feel like vomiting, and don't understand what's happening outside me and how I'm connected with the events. In these situations I benefit from anchoring – if I'm just quick enough to start using the method before I fall.

RECOVERY IS POSSIBLE

Physical activity and any movement in my body are the anchors that work for me. Even the smallest movement – for example, wriggling my toes – is useful, but hard, sweaty gymnastics is the most effective anchor. When my body works, I exist. I'm also very sensitive to sounds. People's voices and chatting with others generally help me. Often, I also benefit from other sounds in the environment; concentrating on them and describing them aloud calms me: I hear the air conditioner buzz and the dishwasher gurgle, so I'm here and everything's fine. Sight is my weakest sense. I can see only with my left eye, so I don't have stereo vision, and this concrete physical limitation makes sight a bad anchor for me.

In terms of anchors, individuals differ a great deal. The crucial thing is to find out what will bring you back to the here and now. For example, many people carry a small stone that they can twiddle, and sometimes I carry photos of people who are close to me or lozenges that I can suck on. Other useful things for me are flavoured lip balms and painting my nails in different colours. They can help me realise that I'm a 34-year-old adult now and no longer a seven-year-old girl under torture.

With progress in my therapy, I've gradually discovered the human qualities of a person with normal feelings in me. I'm happy to be able to cry. One of my most cherished memories is the moment when I burst into tears because of a friend's troubles. On the other hand, I also recognise raging, angry people in me who would like to kill everyone around them with an axe. This is scary, but fortunately I can trust the common sense of my adult self. My behaviour seldom attracts anyone's attention, and I can hide even extreme feelings of hatred behind a smile. I dream that one day I'll be able to act in a completely normal way: be cheerful about cheerful things and sad about sad things. In therapy, I've become aware that hating is not wrong, either. I've been subjected to evil things, so you're goddamn right I'm angry, and it's not wrong to say it. Yet it's difficult for me, as I'm really an overnice doormat that lives for other people. I'll even serve people I actually hate and despise.

A FLOCK GONE ASTRAY

I'm convinced that in my case the continuing sexual violence was enabled by the religious community. Maybe those evil men were not literally protected, but the community's belief that men of God are sacred made the adults who bore the responsibility close their eyes. Naturally, God's own men wouldn't touch children in that way. The truth in all its grubbiness was there on the altar for anyone to see, and the smallest ones of the flock were crying for help, but no one saw or heard. The difference between adults and children is that children see the world as it really is, while adults see just what they presume to be true.

Whether the congregation was responsible for the abuse is a complex issue. Of course, no one in the community was encouraged to behave this way, and most of the members would never have accepted it. Striving for complete sexual purity was the norm, and that's the mistake the community made, and still makes. If even masturbation is considered a sin and all daily things are considered religious issues, someone may confuse apples and oranges. Touching a woman is a sin, but children aren't mentioned, are they? The religious phenomena of fundamentalist circles and the promise of a new beginning nurtured by them attract people whose minds have been shaken, and, in their case, being spiritual versus not being spiritual, being religious versus not being religious will manifest itself in terrible ways.

In addition to the demonisation of sexuality, power relations were a problem. Indeed, congregations are typically areas in which financial crooks and other swindlers can run wild. If you believe that the leader has received his mandate from God, it's difficult for an ordinary rank-and-file member of the community to question his suitability or honesty. Trumpeting judgement and salvation and acting as the representative of God on Earth satisfies the needs of people who may suffer from a range of personality disorders. "Enemies" – that is, people who are too outspoken or ask difficult questions – can then be driven out of the community, into exile, for sowing discord and acting in the wrong spirit. I'm not saying anything about the existence of God; neither do I claim that all religious people are evil – on the contrary – but it's a fact that many evil pastors still continue to run wild in God's name.

Religious issues have slowed down my recovery to a great extent, hindering me from making progress in therapy. It's a completely different thing to be evil in the eyes of people or yourself than in the eyes of God, and this can only be grasped by those who were raised in religion already as children. When I was little, I imagined that it was God who was doing the awful things to me, and I still haven't managed to let go of this thought. This has multiplied my feeling of being evil and of life being pointless. Unfortunately, I've never found refuge or comfort in religion. On the contrary, I've always faced a steely heaven, a divine silence.

My recovery has been hindered, above all, by the fact that I haven't managed to break free from the demands of religion. I suppose I still think at some level that what happened to me was God's righteous punishment; I was, after all, an evil girl. I'm an evil girl... If I've ever wanted to take my case to court, I've been stopped by the feeling that I'm about to rise up against God himself. On the other hand, it's better for me not to take any legal action, at least for the time being. My fragile psyche couldn't stand to hear the possible suspicions concerning "my spiritual state". Fundamentally, I'm rather rational by nature, and I don't have the need to be swept into any sect. I'm only interested in truth, and I occasionally get a glimpse of such beauty in life that I don't need anything else.

I didn't break with my religious community until about a year ago. I haven't had the resources to seek justice or demand an explanation for what happened. A few of the other girls have tried, without much success. The sick, broken community that threw me to the wolves can still not assume responsibility. Maybe one day this will unleash anger in me, give rise to a terrible rebellion. For the time being, I cannot reach so far: all the darkness is still in me, my faults and failure. I'm not stupid – I know perfectly well whose heart the devil resided in and whose not, but, emotionally, I'm only angry at myself, no one else. There's no room for revenge or even a claim for justice.

I wish that, one day, I might be able to think that God loves me, too. It's difficult to imagine how deep the "truths" you learn as a child are imprinted in your identity. The mind cannot get free even if you know, as an intelligent human being, how irrational they are. Nevertheless, I've recently been able to grasp, at least partly, that the truth about the

God's own men wouldn't touch children in that way. The truth in all its grubbiness was there on the altar for anyone to see, and the smallest ones of the flock were crying for help, but no one saw or heard.

Artwork by Seija

world or eternity may not be as simple as I was taught once. A few weeks ago it really dawned on me for the first time that the violence I went through wasn't my fault, after all. This insight created a brief, intense feeling in me that I would describe as grace.

NO HEALING WITHOUT THERAPY

Going to therapy is essential for a patient with a dissociative disorder. Without therapy it's almost impossible to recover or even cope with daily life. Unfortunately, it's difficult to be granted publicly funded therapy. Mental health services are in a wretched state in Finland. The process of becoming a patient of a psychiatric clinic may take a year; you may be granted a meeting with a nurse treating outpatients every second month, and even if you've just attempted suicide you may only dream of being admitted to a ward. Human dignity is priceless, and every person is worth help just because of his or her humanity, but the cuts in mental health services will cost dear to society, too. It's such a challenge to live with difficult traumas that going to work is often impossible without years of therapy. The Finnish health care system doesn't easily grant the right to receive publicly funded therapy if you are unable to work. How can you be able to work before you've even had a chance to go to therapy? Traumas can't be "cured" in any other way. Taking pills won't solve the problem. One would think that having a person on a disability pension would, in the end, cost more for the state.

Attitudes also need fixing. Mental health problems are not the fault of the individual. I've met impossibly spiteful and disdainful doctors and nurses who are more violently sadistic than you can imagine. There are people in this country who have neither rights nor human dignity. They can be called names and mistreated, and it's often impossible for them to assert their rights or have their voices heard. These people live behind the doors of closed wards, and they have my deepest sympathy.

I guess I'm also one of those who have survived despite the treatment, not because of it. An incorrect diagnosis and antipsychotic medication put my life on hold for years. Dissociative disorder cannot be treated

A smooth rhythm and
safe daily life, as well
as my studies enhance
recovery and provide
room for dealing with
difficult issues

with medication, though some symptoms can be alleviated by selective serotonin reuptake inhibitors (SSRIs), for example. My experience is that antipsychotics just strengthen the feeling of gliding outside yourself. When medication makes you feel numb, you don't recognise your feelings. Many dissociative patients take antipsychotics, which is also a problem in terms of side effects: they can be drastic. Schizophrenics have a deficiency in their brain, a "broken" part, that can be partly repaired by medication. In the case of dissociative disorder, however, medication creates broken parts, muddling the brain chemistry, because there's no psychosis for the medication to treat.

I've been lucky in one way: I was allowed to start therapy as soon as I got the correct diagnosis, so I'm finally getting the right kind of help. I'm in a therapeutic relationship built on trust and confidentiality: all the parts of my personality will be heard and can feel secure. In a way, my past is now becoming familiar to me; it's part of me, and I even accept it. Getting to know the different parts of my personality hasn't been easy; for example, my aggressive, defensive parts cause anxiety in me. For the time being, I don't even dare to dream of integration. A smooth rhythm and safe daily life, as well as my studies, enhance recovery and provide room for dealing with difficult issues.

At present, I talk fairly openly about my experiences. Speaking the truth helps me. It makes my past more real. Should I be ashamed of my childhood and keep quiet about it as if it were my own fault? Or should I open my mouth and tell the truth? As long as everyone keeps silent, the experiences of traumatised people don't exist – and neither does the possibility of getting help. Being honest is hard, because the parts of my personality that are going through the trauma fear being punished for their honesty. Thus, I try to proceed one step at a time, looking for inner security.

THE PSYCHO-PHYSICAL WHOLE

If you suffer from a dissociative disorder, you need to pay attention both to your mental and physical condition. In the worst years of my antipsychotic medication, I weighed 150 kilos, 80 kilos more than now. I also slept eighteen hours a day. I had absolutely no connection with my body, because the bond between the mind and the body was, occasionally, totally broken as a result of forced medication. This made healing completely impossible. The more connections you can create between your mind and body, the less dissociated and isolated you feel.

We all have our own ways of "moving in to live in our bodies". I've benefited from physical activity to a great extent. It's healing to feel your arms and legs function and your heart beat. According to recent studies, one's diet and good intestinal bacteria probably affect the mood more than we know at present, and, in so far as healthy food helps depressed people, for example, it will certainly also help those with a dissociative disorder. When you eat regularly and in a healthy way, your energy level stays even and your body functions properly. Mostly, traumas give you weaker self-esteem. A healthy diet is a way of showing yourself that you deserve good things. You may and should take care of yourself.

I lead a healthy life, but I still keep falling ill easily. I suffer from a cold almost all the time. I suppose it's because my body is constantly in a state of defence. When part of the body is still going through the trauma, there are possible attackers everywhere. There's not enough energy to defend the body against viruses and bacteria. I also suffer continually from severe muscular tension and problems with digestion. It's difficult, and even feels dangerous, to relax.

Alcohol and cannabis are definitely a bad choice if you have a dissociative disorder. Everything that draws you away from your body and clear thinking will be harmful. Traumas predispose you to self-harm and numbing your inner self, so you may want to be careful with intoxicants. This is not always easy. When things are at their worst, you'll want to quit existing; you'll want to turn the lights off.

CLOSING WORDS

I now believe that I'll survive. In addition to studying, I work part-time, do a great deal of physical activity and reading, go to therapy and have a good social network. I'll become a steady tax-payer and an ordinary person. My past often seems like a nightmare.

But it is there, even if it lies dormant from time to time. I guess it will take me my whole life to learn to cope with myself, with "me and my head". Yet, a journey into the self can be fun, too. It's nice to learn to live. Today is the only day of my only life, and I decide how I will live it and how I will treat myself and others today. I believe that life itself will carry me. It's a vacation from eternal non-existence, a unique opportunity to experience, feel and succeed. Of course, it also gives you the possibility of failing and spoiling everything, but, even so, even at its worst, it's unique and irreplaceable. There will hardly be a second chance.

You'll have a happy life if you can work and love. Perhaps it was Freud who said that. It's important to have a flame in your life, and you can find it by taking charge. No one will give or offer you this control over your own life: you need to take it.

Artwork by Carita

Inari

My name is Inari. I'm a 33-year-old practical nurse and the mother of a teenage girl; I have a disability pension and am participating in full-time rehabilitation.

I was born to a single mother several years after my siblings. My mother's older children moved to the other side of the country when I was small, and I was left alone with my mother. She was cruel to me. Physical violence, subjugation and isolation were everyday methods of child-rearing in our family. My childhood was also overshadowed by belonging to a religious community which, through fear, kept a tight grip on its members.

My mother struggled with her health during her youth. She had neurological diseases and clearly suffered from mental health problems with which she never wanted any help. Things could blow up at home at any time. I tried to make myself as invisible as possible and not get under my mother's feet, because she could lose her temper at any moment. At times, I was even told to keep away, so I spent a great deal of time in my room and in the shed outside the house. I felt and was told that I was an unwanted pain in the neck.

I was also brought up in a small, narrow-minded religious community. My mother no longer went to the meetings of the community, but made me attend them regularly. I'd like to think that maybe my mother thought I'd learn a good set of values there and stay away from mischief. In fact, I learned to be afraid and keep secrets.

I'd been taught to have a religious outlook on life already as a child, so I wasn't able to question it. It also kept me safe. I wasn't hurt by being bullied at school, as I'd been told that real believers would be persecuted. I just felt bad for my schoolmates who, being infidels, would end up in eternal damnation.

I lost myself in the world of religion. I looked for acceptance there and, at the same time, I had a chance to get away from home. But I felt all the time that nothing was good enough for God. He could read my mind and knew even if I sinned just in my thoughts. I did everything as correctly as I could, but I already felt damned. The thought that God knew even my sinful thoughts haunted me. When I was six, I tried to commit suicide by walking in front of a train. I knew it was wrong, but I felt that I was just a nuisance to everybody.

Generally, the members of the religious community were considered to be good, law-abiding and honourable people. But in a small circle behind this facade of decency, terrible things took place. Together with his friend, a high-ranking member of the community engaged in the sexual abuse of children. This was a secret known to only a few people, and I still don't know how widely the members of the congregation knew about it. For us, these men were the representatives of God on Earth whose deeds could not be questioned.

I had already been turned into a perfect victim. I was lonely and scared, I craved to be accepted and I knew how to keep quiet. I could be kept silent through threats and intimidation. I tried to talk about what had happened, once in the religious community and once at home. I was punished for both attempts. I was told that no-one would believe me and I'd suffer for the rest of my life if I told anyone. I still haven't got over this idea.

The sexual abuse ended when I reached puberty. Instead of feeling relieved, I felt rejected. At the same time, I began to question the teachings of religion as a result of secretly getting to know people outside the community. I had psychogenic symptoms and was self-destructive and angry. In my teens, I was admitted to a psychiatric ward for the first time. During my stay there I found enough courage to break away from the religious community. I announced that I would refuse to return home and live with my mother. I still didn't dare to talk about what had happened in my childhood, but they noticed on the ward that something was wrong at home. I was allowed to move out.

As a teenager, I kept running away. I liked travelling, sitting on a train or a bus, though I seldom planned where to stay at the end of the trip. I often slept outside or in unsafe places. During adolescence, I again became a victim of sexual abuse. The circumstances were in many ways familiar: a small, closed group, a charismatic leader, secrets. After these events, I tried to commit suicide. I felt that nothing but horrible things happened to me and that I was destined to fail.

I began to find myself in places I didn't recognise and forget who I was. I thought that there was something wrong with my head, as there were gaps in my memory. I questioned the teachings of religion, but still felt that I was possessed by demons. I began to doubt my childhood memories. I thought that I was crazy and had invented everything.

#I am safe now.

#I will also be breathing tomorrow.

My smartphone functions as my multimedia diary about my life with dissociative disorder and a pocket journal with my collection of anchors.

Muista eläÄ päivittäin

#Remember to live. Every day!

FOREVE

Artwork by Seija

I spent my adolescence in an institution, suffering from a variety of symptoms. I was self-destructive, often went berserk and kept running away. However, I also found hobbies that I liked, got to know new people, and became more interested in going to school. I blocked out my past, thinking that I had made it. At the age of eighteen, I had a job and was engaged and pregnant.

I'm amazed that I could cope for such a long time, leading an almost normal family life – considering how unfamiliar it was for me. I had a family, friends, hobbies and a job, and I was also studying. I was fine. I was enjoying my life, but kept pushing myself harder and harder. I piled up work and obligations for myself.

The childhood scenes seemed more and more distant all the time, and I began again to doubt whether they had even taken place. However, meeting one of my abusers made past scenes resurface in my mind.

I noticed that my memory was beginning to fail in my everyday life. I found myself in places I didn't know and in curious situations in the midst of strangers. I didn't want to stop to think what was going on, but kept performing more than ever – until I was exhausted.

At the age of twenty-five, I was put on sick leave because of burnout and depression. My symptoms increased and intensified rapidly. I suffered from anxiety and insomnia, was afraid of social situations, and had obsessive thoughts and compulsive symptoms. However, I was able to function fairly normally every second week when my daughter lived with me. I was given several diagnoses and heavy medication.

I was confused about my symptoms, though I also understood that my childhood hadn't been exactly normal. I had decided to keep quiet about what had happened in my childhood – until the statute of limitations on the offences expired. I felt that I had to do that for my own security.

A few months after I started sick leave, I ended up on a psychiatric ward. During the following five years, I spent as much time in hospital as at home. I was suicidal; I often felt safe from myself only when I was in limb restraints in the hospital. My daughter went to live with her father.

At regular intervals, I had new symptoms and got new diagnoses and new medication. At the same time, I became physically ill, suffering from diverse symptoms.

I now feel that I was driven forward by my self-destructive impulses. My mind was constantly drawing up plans for the next suicide attempt. I hurt myself impulsively and systematically. Sometimes I wondered how I had ended up in a situation where I had hurt myself – and asked for help.

It seemed that those treating me were all at sea. Doctors, nurses and wards changed. Often, I came to the ward via the emergency room, because of my suicidal behaviour. It bothers me that perhaps my symptoms were never seen as a whole; instead, those treating me concentrated on dealing with the acute situation.

My suicide attempts became more serious. When I was twenty-nine, I ran away from the psychiatric ward and jumped off a third-floor balcony. In addition to broken bones and nerve damage, the accident left me with chronic pains from which I still suffer. I couldn't move without a wheelchair or cope with everyday life without daily help. During the following years, I went through several operations and periods of rehabilitation.

The hospital became a refuge and a nightmare for me. I could hardly stand any kind of medical treatment or physical contact with other people. The future seemed hopeless.

After my jump, I was moved to another psychiatric clinic – one with more expertise in traumatisation and dissociation. There they asked me for the first time whether I had had a traumatic past, and I was ready to talk about it. They cut back on my medication and gave me trauma therapy. Gradually, I began to recover.

I needed help and supervision in my daily life, so I moved to an assisted living unit. Every few weeks, I went to the hospital, either in accordance with my treatment plan or because of a critical situation. My room on the psychiatric ward became my first refuge.

Severe depression and my suicidal tendencies were still a challenge during my healing process. It was hard to believe that I could ever feel better. At times, I felt there was hope, but it disappeared quickly when

I found myself pouring boiling water on myself or cutting my wrists. Nevertheless, my condition improved little by little, and from time to time I began to feel safe at home, too.

I joined an online peer support group for people with dissociative disorders, and it improved my condition at least as much as professional treatment did. I had always felt like an outsider and a strange bird, so it was wonderful to find out that other people had similar experiences, symptoms and feelings! I heard about good experiences of therapy and rehabilitation, and I began to have slight hopes that I, too, might have them one day. Because of their own experiences, the members of this group understood me much better than my other friends and the professionals who treated me.

I gradually got better, but two years ago there was a dramatic change. I went to hospital for a small keyhole operation, in which serious mistakes were made that almost killed me. I was kept in an induced coma for weeks in a critical state in an intensive care unit. When I started to come around and understood what had happened, I was scared. Though earlier I had tried seriously to commit suicide several times, I was really happy to be alive. When I woke up, the first thing I saw was the worry and the distress of my family – something I had never noticed in all those years of self-destruction. During my recovery in hospital I saw my life in a new light and made important decisions: for example, my self-destruction had to come to an end.

As my depression yielded, I became motivated to work on recovery. I had already gone to therapy for a few years and learned alternative ways of controlling anxiety and dissociative states. I had great faith that I would recover one day: I got help from professionals, peers and friends. For the first time in ten years I made plans for my future.

Healing began with things that are really very simple such as learning to eat, sleep and stick to good daily routines. My life, which had felt chaotic for years, got a rhythm that helped me fight against my dissociative states.

I also made rapid progress with physical recovery. It felt good and increased my motivation greatly. A year after the unfortunate operation, I was able to get rid of the wheelchair. When I started to move, it was possible to decrease the heavy medication. My memory and concentration improved, and I was able to return to my studies.

The more time passes, the more certain I am that I will make it. However, at the same time I'm waiting for the first big relapse in my recovery, afraid that I will find myself back in a vortex of self-destruction and periods spent in hospital.

To a great extent, I still feel guilty for and ashamed of what happened in my childhood. Though I understand that children can't be held responsible for the wrongs that are done to them, I keep thinking about what I could have done to prevent or stop those events. Those evil people knew how to manipulate my sense of guilt when they kept telling me that I was to blame for everything.

Fear and guilt made me keep silent for a long time even as an adult. It seems odd that the statute of limitations on these crimes expires so soon: it can take much longer for the victim to be able to talk about what happened.

My future looks bright. I still struggle with dissociative states every day and have a great deal to work on in therapy, but things are improving little by little. Carefully, I've started to plan my future, continued my studies and found new friends. My daughter, who is now moving in with me again, is my greatest delight. I'm grateful to have a chance, once again, to share my everyday life with her.

Carita

When I was sitting in my first therapy
session, I couldn't even guess
what a journey I was setting out on.

Therapy was hard work; it meant using methods that were slow and strange to me, but I managed to keep going. Because I had decided not to quit. I had also decided to cut all contact with my parents. At the time, I didn't yet recognise the things or deeds that had broken me. I didn't realise that the things I had gone through were bad enough to break me. Now, twelve years later, I'm a 34-year-old mother of two children. Therapy has given me tools for creating a sense of security, so that the different parts of my fragmented personality have had the courage to integrate with the inner community that is also known as me. At the same time, I've been building my external life, attaining a balance. One of the biggest circles of my life has been closed, but growth goes on. I am now strong enough to carry the heavy load of my mind and to step out of my past. This is my brief story about my journey to integration and to recovery from a trauma-induced dissociative disorder.

These were the words with which I stepped in front of people for the first time:

THE WAR IN SYRIA. MY WAR.

For years, I've reflected on how to come out with this issue. Or why. What would my story mean to others, and what would the consequences be?

Would I tell my story purely for egotistical reasons, or is helping others my greatest motivation? Would coming out be above all connected with my need to be seen, heard and understood? Would anyone believe me, and would it even matter? How should I tell my story; where would I begin?

Probably I've been hindered mostly by fear and shame, but I've also been hampered by a sound measure of discretion. Nowadays I have an instinct for self-protection. I don't want my trauma to define everything I do, but I also know that this world will not get any better if I keep silent. Everything leads to a reaction. You can never be prepared for everything. You can't foresee everything.

I'm a wife and a mother. I was going to write that I'm a rather ordinary wife and mother, but that may not be quite true: in addition to these identities, I have several other identities, too. I have a dissociative disorder: to be more specific, a dissociative identity disorder.

My dissociative identity disorder is a result of my being a victim of neglect, assault and abuse from very early in life. We moved often, so the adults with whom I came into contact didn't notice my distress. I've counted that I switched to a new school seven times in primary school alone. Those people who momentarily saw my distress looked the other way.

I was bullied in many schools, and the older I became, the more sadistic the methods of bullying were. In lower secondary school, "bullying" assumed at worst features of mental and physical torture. There was a lot of sexual abuse. At home, I didn't get the weapons to defend myself. It's no wonder I couldn't do it. When you grow up in an abnormal environment, you can't know where to draw the line. You easily end up being an object. Many people would say about my childhood: "How can you ever recover from that?"

I've gone to trauma therapy for more than ten years, and will probably continue for many more years. But the worst part is over now. There's cooperation between the different parts of my fragmented self. One sign of this is that I don't have memory breaks, or gaps in my memory, as often as I used to. I don't panic or fly into a rage anymore. I know how to protect myself. I don't get depressed anymore when difficult emotions resurface. It's been a few years since the last time I wished for a silent death.

I used to compare myself to other people, and saw only differences. Now I notice similarities and shared features. Gradually, the parts of me that bear the agonising feelings and experiences caused by traumatic scenes are returning and becoming part of my core consciousness; together, we can move on and leave the traumatic period behind. I'm on the way to healing, and it now seems possible to think that, one day, the dissociative identity disorder will be part of my past.

I don't want to get rid of the disorder because I hate or am ashamed of it, though I've sometimes felt that way, too. I feel deep empathy and gratefulness for my dissociation. It kept me alive and functional in unbearable circumstances. It held my hand when no-one else comforted me. It has been my superpower and companion on this journey, but its task has now been fulfilled. We don't live in constant danger and fear anymore. I'm an adult with a family of my own now. It's my turn to provide my own children with the security I never had. I will not succeed in this task if part of me continues to live in another time, a period of constant warfare. It's time to accept, give thanks and continue the journey together. As one me.

For years, I've carried this question with me: "What turns a human being into a monster?" The answer has always been just around the corner, but it has only become clear in my mind in the past few years. I couldn't find the answer until I had faced the "monster" in me. I had to take it in my arms and embrace it. I had to tell it that everything was fine now; I had to comfort it. I had to make food and build a nest for it. I had to learn to love it and see it the way it really is. It was the hardest thing I've ever done.

Trauma is a disease that extends across generations. A child is born innocent. A child is never guilty of the evil that happens. A child adapts and learns to cope. I've had to reflect a great deal on the hypothetical reasons why my parents – both of them – failed in their task in my case. What were the terrible experiences on which their own inner traumatic children had got stuck? And what kind of horrors had their parents gone through in the war?

Over the years, I've managed to collect a few pieces of information on my parents' lives and, from them, formed a picture that makes sense. I'm sorry for their inner children. I feel great empathy for their experiences. I can understand, but I can't forgive the adults who broke me. And though I can't forgive the ones who did evil things to me, I want to offer my quiet acceptance to the ones who are willing to change. It's never too late. There's always room for spiritual growth.

This will end with me. I'm offering my children the kind of childhood I also should have had. I've been given a great opportunity to raise nice, strong and coherent men into this world. The kind of good people that this age needs. I'm extremely grateful for this possibility and proud of myself for having had the strength to do all the work that has made this possible.

This age, our time, occasionally seems desperately difficult and frightening. There are threats in the air. The war in Syria, the flood of refugees, mass extinctions, climate change. All the horrible things that are happening right now in Aleppo, for example. At this very moment, in front of our eyes, the same things that have taken place here in Finland are happening: new traumas, diseases and vortexes of horrors are being created.

Recently, I watched the documentary Faces of the Syrian War. I was brought up short by it. The documentary presents a stark, grotesque picture of Aleppo. It gives new meaning to many Finnish words. Culturally, we Syrians and Finns are very far apart, but, through humanitarian deeds and the survival mechanisms of the human species, our connections and similarities have become as obvious as a huge exclamation mark. From my school days, I remember lessons when we dealt with the wars in which Finland has been involved. In those lessons, our wars somehow seemed cleaner, nobler and more honourable than the wars waged by other countries. I don't recall that we ever talked about the war crimes committed in Finland. Only now have we Finns started to deal with this darker side of Finland's history. The things we hear about our past are as terrible as the things that are taking place in Syria and Iraq now. Thank you, Niklas Meltio, for the work you do and for this documentary. I can only imagine the wounds you have in your soul: without them, you might not be making such documentaries. Thank you for your sacrifice.

The thought of all this makes me feel desperate. At first thought, it seems that I have no strength. But there is also something different in this age. Something new. We know a great deal more. We all have our voices, and we have channels through which to make them heard. Trauma lives off secrecy. It gains force in silence. I can make a difference by telling my story. There are many brave people who have come out with their stories now. I want to thank them. Through my contribution, I am joining this group of people. Thus, my story is not unique. And that's where its magic lies. I want everyone to know that no-one is too broken to survive and recover.

HIDING IN A PLACE EVERYONE CAN SEE

When I was asked about my childhood at the beginning of my therapy, I always answered the same way: "My early childhood was like a bed of roses, and my problems didn't start until I was in my teens. I was a terrible teenager." This was also a sentence that would make my parents nod approvingly when I visited them. Of course, that's how it was. Or was it?

We lived in a big house near Helsinki. My father was the managing director of a big company, and my mother spent the days with me. Our house was a three-storey building, and the middle and the upper floor were connected by a long spiral staircase. I remember my mother vacuuming at the upper end of the stairs, and I was playing on the stairs below her. The vacuum cleaner was big. It was one of those high, round, cylinder-like things. It was blue and grey. Did my mother get annoyed with the child who was climbing up the stairs and wouldn't keep away though she was told to do so? A question I will probably never get an answer to. In her anger, my mother kicked the vacuum cleaner into me so that I fell down those high stairs. I was in terrible pain but alive. My arm hurt badly. My small mind couldn't cope with the moment when my mother dashed down the stairs and was again the gentle mother who took me in her arms and comforted me: it broke my mind. I split. I became Number One, who carries this bitter scene in herself. And Number Two, who watches the scene with no emotion whatsoever. And Number Three, who continues living as if nothing has happened. I still remember what the splitting felt like.

For decades, I remembered something completely different. I remembered the vacuum-cleaner, but not my mother. I remembered that in some odd way I tripped on the stairs and rolled down, but wasn't hurt at all. It was as if I was wrapped in some pink gauze through which the world seemed slightly ethereal, moving in slow-motion. Everything was like a dream. Later, when I told my mother what I had felt, she told me that our house was haunted and I was the only one who could see the ghost. So in one way or another, the scene was connected with this ghost.

In the basement of our big house, we had a sauna, a swimming pool

Artwork by Carita

and a bar. This floor especially was haunted. It was a frightening place where terrible things happened, for example, with my father. After this event, a ghost followed our family wherever we moved. Of course, I didn't know anything about dissociation at the time. Not until I went to therapy as a young adult did I hear the term for the first time, and, even then, it took several years before I really understood what it meant.

Already as a small child, I liked to do my own thing. I would go roaming alone in the woods at the age of four. At our cabin, our dogs would sometimes follow me. I remember that I was happy about the dogs being there, because then the wolves wouldn't eat me in the forest. You could sometimes get a glimpse of them near our cabin. Still, I wasn't afraid of being in the forest. But there were other things I was afraid of. The adults often had parties and slept in late at the cabin. In the morning I would come downstairs. I climbed on the table by the sink and opened the upper cupboard. I knew where the cocoa jar was. There was a feeding bottle in the next cupboard, but I didn't take it. My mother had said that a fly had pooed in it. It bothered me a bit, but having a stomach full of cocoa powder comforted me. I was very independent and quite brave at a very young age. I had to be. However, I was often really scared and needed my mother badly. I remember how I woke up with a terrible call of nature one morning. I brought the potty next to my parents' bed. They were sleeping and I didn't manage to wake up my mother. I relieved myself in the potty and tried once more to wake my mother, but she didn't wake up. She didn't even stir. Our dog Ira took care of me. First she ate up the content of the potty and then licked me clean.

My fingers got shut in the car door surprisingly often. "Oh, how stupid of me to leave my hand there again!" As an adult I've understood that it wasn't my fault that my mother shut the door too quickly. My mind couldn't understand that my mother hurt me intentionally. I remember how automatically I thought that I was being clumsy. I completely ignored what had really happened. The act of ignoring was not conscious: it was like a biological automatic reaction.

We often had parties in which the guests consisted mostly of my father's colleagues. At these parties, my father – usually so distant – made me his doll and was very cheerful. The adults found it amusing when cigar smoke made me cough and the bitter taste of whisky made me grimace. Pretending to be precocious, I whispered funny-sounding questions in the ears of the adults. But I also learned something useful at those parties. I internalised table etiquette and good manners at an early age.

I often had nightmares and sleepwalked. The nightmares were frequently about the same themes: for example, my parents having to abandon me because of some catastrophe. The dreams left me with a paralysing depression. We had to install latches on the outside doors because I often tried to go outside when sleepwalking. Once I was found in our front yard in winter, in pyjamas and sound asleep. I would wake up frantic and wet my bed almost every night. When I started school, I had to stay after school already in first grade, because I was late almost every morning.

We moved often. I've counted that, just at primary level, I went to seven different schools, including two schools abroad. No-one noticed my distress, though I hid messages in my drawings and paintings. Sometimes I was deeply anxious when sitting in the classroom. I felt that I couldn't stay awake or understand what the teacher was trying to teach us. Sometimes when this happened, I said that I felt ill or had a headache so that I could get away. I also had a great deal of physical symptoms. I frequently had mysterious headaches or stomach aches. They ran tests on me, but never found any medical reason for the pain.

INHERITING A TRAUMA
Every child is born into this world innocent

As part of my therapeutic journey, I have reflected on such fundamental questions as what makes a human being evil. What makes a parent hurt his or her own child ruthlessly? Why didn't I turn out evil? Am I evil, too?

When they were still children my grandparents on my mother's side were torn cruelly from their roots in Karelia in the thick of the war in Finland. My grandfather was sent to Sweden as a war child. My father's mother came from Ostrobothnia and served at the front in the women's auxiliary forces. She raised her bastard son in the fear and admonition of the Lord. We seldom talked about the past, but, over the years, I've managed to gather bits of information from here and there; from them, I've formed an understandable picture of the kind of wounds my grandparents bore. The world was very different then. From my grandparents, my parents inherited the wounds caused by the war, handing them down to me, too.

Things have not always been just evil. We've also had periods of ordinary family life. Many beautiful experiences and even dear memories. But it's been a split life. A double life. I'm sure it's difficult to imagine what kind of deeds can be hidden behind charming smiles.

There were many things in my parents' behaviour that I also recognise in my behaviour. I'm sure that my parents also suffered from disso-

Four generations.

ciative disorder, but the difference is that they never sought or got help for their disorders. After understanding this, I feel empathy for their suffering, but I can't forgive them. And I don't need to. I've learned that understanding is the crucial and liberating thing, but it is not a synonym for acceptance. Understanding leads to growth. I've also learned to accord this same understanding to myself. As I try to understand, I can choose differently.

PSYCHOLOGICAL VIOLENCE

My mother raised me to become a witch, binding me to herself in that way.

I've always taken it for granted that my father was evil. I knew it. My mother's evil doings were somehow more complicated in my mind. It has been unbearable to me that, as parents, both of them failed me. I was left with no sense of security.

I didn't belong to any religious community as a child, but religion and faith in all their manifestations have always interested, captivated and even frightened me. With all their rules and patterns of behaviour, they have always felt restrictive and unfair. They have imposed on me a mould in which I've never been able to fit. But there was nothing wrong with the mould: I was the problem. That's what I was often told, both at home and elsewhere.

The educational tradition of the Lutheran Church of Finland includes participation in a confirmation camp where young people are taught religious matters. When I went to confirmation camp, I took along all the academic journals I had collected on the Christian faith and the rebellious teen-age Warrior: the trigger-happy me with my fully loaded gun. On top of this, I happened to choose a parish the pastor of which was extremely conservative and took the Word literally. He quit before the camp was over.

I left home very young – a broken youth with no resources to cope with the everyday life of an adult. This meant that, at times, I had no home, and, when I did have one, there was usually nothing else but the light and some mould in the fridge. The social services offices said they "couldn't" help me, but sometimes – when I was almost starving – I asked for assistance at the office of the parish. They would send a lady to the shop with me, and for a while there would be some food in my fridge. It was terribly embarrassing, but I'll be grateful to this lady all my life. So good things also happen, and usually there's really more good than bad in life. However, it's essential that we make the evil visible so that we can get rid of it. So that we can grow as human beings.

Outwardly, we looked like ordinary nominal Lutherans. But weird things went on in our family. My mother has always been extremely interested in witchcraft, and she tried to raise me to do the same. She tried to make me a witch. She kept telling me that all the women of our family had an instinct for witchcraft. The blame for many wounds and odd events was put on ghosts and demons. Sometimes my mother could even growl like a devil who had emerged from Hell. Alcohol, and perhaps even her own history of trauma, played a part in this matter.

I've come to think that this Witch in my mother was a part that she had created in order to protect herself, as she told me that this power of hers was something no man could destroy. The only one who could destroy her was me. In my young mind, this statement turned into an inner contradiction. Part of me felt proud and omnipotent: "I am the most powerful Witch of all!" Then again, part of me felt guilty and ashamed: "Ugh, what an awful person I am! I must be incredibly evil to want to destroy my own mother!" All the while my inner self was screaming in despair: "This is wrong! This is wrong! Don't listen!" The chaos and split in me grew stronger. This sounds completely mad, and, in fact, it is. When we are faced with such nonsense as adults, we know how to protect ourselves from it, but if you've been raised in an abnormal, harmful environment, you can't – as a child – do anything but change your inner world to correspond to the outer world. This is an involuntary biological phenomenon the purpose of which is to guarantee survival. You have to attach yourself to your parents even if they hurt you. This is a scientific fact. Nevertheless, a tiny part of us understands that something is wrong. "This is wrong!" I understood that I didn't have any magical skills and that I was being told lies. Still, part of me railed at myself for being such a miserable failure that not even the gift of witchcraft – which was generations old – had been passed down to me. In addition, I was evil

Of course, the purpose of all this was to control me. In this way, my mother bound me to herself and her distorted world. That way, she was not alone. When I became more independent and began to question things aloud, the loop was tightened by saying that I was free to choose between my family and the rest of the world. What an impossible choice! Either way, I would be left alone and outside; I would be isolated. I was between a rock and a hard place. It was totally absurd.

Making me live in a world of witches was an extremely destructive form of violence the consequences of which are still not visible to other people. This has been such a difficult thing and a complex knot that I couldn't start to talk about it in therapy until a few years ago. It's been difficult to work on traumas caused by physical violence, but this witch issue is, in terms of the gamut of difficulty, right at the top along with sexual abuse. Working on traumas is also difficult because my family members never admitted that I was mistreated. Usually everyone just behaved as if nothing had happened. As a result, you start to doubt whether those things ever even took place. The scenes may stay in your mind as images, but the feelings connected with them are suppressed. A child's mind goes over these impossible, wounding situations again and again. The mind breaks into pieces. Things are buried in the depths of the subconscious. A time bomb has been set. About ten years ago I had the opportunity to wonder about this to my mother over the phone, and she used freedom of religion as her defence. It sounds sick and absurd. And criminal! Doesn't it?

But exactly the same mechanism is applied in some widely accepted and active religious communities. Unbelievable!

I still don't belong to any religious community, but I do consider myself a highly spiritual person. I've created various rituals for myself, but they have no mystical purpose. As far as I've observed, rituals and their creation are part of the species-typical behaviour of humans. They are a way of giving rhythm to life and taking spiritual needs into consideration. A way of meditating and pausing to consider things. A continuation of routines, or something that gives you a break from them. Love, a sense of wellness and being together with the family are intimately connected with these rituals. Here in Finland, nature works in the same way as belonging to a church. We are empowered, go on retreats and experience unity there. When I sit by a campfire, I sometimes beat on a frame drum I've built myself. The rhythm and vibration of the drum take me quickly to a meditative state which, when the conditions are right, calms me down. I want to learn to feel good in my body and mind. I may sing and hum. For me, spirituality and its manifestations are a very delicate and personal thing. Though earlier I rebelled against everything that had to do with spirituality, I now refrain from commenting on other people's ways of expressing it. Nevertheless, I've often been the target of their comments and even judgments.

I dream of being part of a community in which I could realise myself in this way, together with like-minded people, and thus get a sense of belonging and well-being and of love. Are these not the basic ideas behind the birth of religion? For me, this dream contains nothing that is "supernatural", mystical and regular. And that's good. When I was younger, I was categorically against everything that had to do with religion, and I wasn't afraid to use my voice. No wonder, when you think of all the ways in which I had been broken. I'm not afraid of making my opinion heard even now, but, with a curious and open mind, I'm also more flexible as concerns my own truth; I now see things from a number of perspectives and am, therefore, more thoughtful when opening my mouth. My circle of friends and acquaintances consists of a range of kindred spirits and believers.

Nevertheless, I strongly feel that we interfere all too seldom with the psychological and physical violence that goes on in religious communities. We should also discuss how to protect children better in this respect – even by law and through legal measures.

CRIME AND PUNISHMENT

It seems strange to think about justice. What is it? How is it realised? Is there any such thing?

I've never confronted my parents concerning the way I was treated. There have been a few rare contacts by phone or letter, but we've never met since I broke off my relationship with them and started going to therapy.

I've submitted a few requests for a police investigation in vain. They've been retraumatising experiences. The cold, hard and suspicious attitude of the police officer when he wrote down my story was too much for my fragile mind. When I came out of one of the hearings, I had a massive panic attack for which, fortunately, I got professional and gentle help quickly from a crisis centre nearby. Recovering from the experience took years. Not even the police were safe for me.

This happened at a time when the Finnish law on child abuse was being revised. Earlier, the sexual abuse of a child was a crime for which the statute of limitations expired after ten years. Since the change, the ten-year-period does not begin until the child turns eighteen. However, in my case the statute of limitations for my parents' crimes had already expired, because, in Finland, one can't be sued on the basis of a revised law for crimes that were committed under an earlier law. Logical? Not in my opinion.

My case was also difficult to investigate because our family had moved so much. The local police can't investigate things that have happened in the neighbouring province: they have to request executive assistance from the authorities in the other place.

Though the legal reform is clearly a step in the right direction, it is still very problematic and not comprehensive enough. However, I don't want to use the space available in this book to discuss that issue. I'm also not the right person to evaluate what kind of punishment my parents should get for their crimes from the point of view of justice. The day when my mind opened its darkest and deepest layers to me and I stepped out of there as a coherent me, carrying my worst experiences in my arms, I understood that nothing can compensate for the crime of which I had been a victim. There is no justice for me in this life.

I'm not the only victim of my father. Thus, it's totally incomprehensible that my father can walk free and carry out his inclinations without any hindrance though there are many people who say they have had the kind of experiences I've had and though it's generally known that he has a propensity for beastliness. Maybe part of the problem is that the issue is so vast and such a disgusting taboo that no-one wants to have anything to do with it. How can a parent be so cruel to his own child, or any child? Or are we dealing with something that is part of our culture? Honour your mother and father no matter what. That's what my father kept telling me, and I'm sure it's something that he was also told. Keep quiet. Honour and bow down. Just grit your teeth and you'll survive.

THE WRONG KIND

All my life, I've been the wrong kind of person. I wasn't good enough for my parents, so how could I be good enough for myself? Other people and things that have to do with my appearance have always determined what I should be like.

My father considered me very beautiful but commented unkindly on my eating habits, saying that I was going to get fat and be disgusting. At school my appearance attracted the attention of boys, because my breasts developed early and I wore tight shirts. Over the years, many of my boyfriends made comments on the parts of my body they weren't happy with. One thought my legs were too short, and another one said that my eyes were too far apart. It's disturbing to what extent I've been objectified. I've been treated like a thing! And I've let it happen, because I haven't seen my own value nor been able to defend myself properly.

How in the world can anyone think that commenting on someone's appearance in any way other than constructively can ever be justified?

That is why some parts of my personality identify strongly with the male gender. Deep inside, they believe that women are weak. "Women and girls can be mistreated and abused." "Women can't be taken seriously or considered proficient." This is really sad, but understandable if we

Artwork by Carita

It has been tough to look at photos of my childhood. They show people who broke me, making painful memories surface. Not just in me, but also in the minds of my family members. This has meant that there's always been an uneasy silence when I've tried to look at photos from the time when I was a child with anyone from my family. Even in my photos, my childhood is covered in a shroud of silent shame and secrecy.

look at my world of experiences.

ME AND MY MEMORY

Of my dissociation-related symptoms probably the most visible one for the outside world is my faulty or unreliable memory. Or perhaps my memory works fine and I just have memory gaps because my personality is fragmented into parts between which experiences, feelings and memories are not shared.

I often misplace things, and if I haven't written down engagements in my calendar, I'm sure to forget them. Undoubtedly, this is also a result of the fact that maintaining inner consensus and calming the constant tumult in my mind requires a great deal of mental energy. My energy resources are limited, and often too small.

I've been to family parties where I remember or recognise only my closest family members though I've actually known most of the guests for years. Connecting names and faces is generally difficult for me.

We all have a range of roles in our everyday lives – think of the different people we are at home and at work. For me, this division of roles has just been much more concrete. My experiences, memories, feelings, features and even gender can be different depending on which one of my parts is "in charge".

Though I've become split many times, there are a few parts of me that are more distinctly present in my everyday life, and each of them fulfils a special task. In my adult life, the switch between parts has produced awkward situations: for example, the experiences of one part can't be shared by the other parts of my personality. I don't necessarily recognise the people I meet at work when I'm not working. My memory is so unreliable that people think that I am neglectful or just don't care. I don't always have the energy to correct such views, but I can guarantee that this is not the case. Actually, I often try to compensate for the way my memory works by overperforming and punishing myself inwardly.

I AM NOT ILL

I don't consider my dissociative disorder a disease. It's a normal way for the mind to react in an unbearable situation. It's a survival mechanism which has enabled me to continue leading a normal life despite the traumatising things I've experienced. In early childhood, it had a protective purpose, but, as I've grown, it has started to work against me. Constant splitting may protect you momentarily in difficult situations, but it doesn't prevent the situations. It's a kind of physical structure, a "defect" in the brain. The good news is that, with proper help, the brain can grow physically coherent.

For me, dissociative disorder is not a disease, but the symptoms caused by it are: depression, a distorted self-image, eating disorders, self-destruction, physical inflammatory pain, dizziness, headaches, and so on.

The parts of me that have been created by dissociation are not part of a disease. They are me.

As a result of my integration, the parts of my personality have not disappeared or died as I was afraid they would do: they are returning to my coherent core self with all their characteristics – both good and bad. Nothing and nobody has been cut out. My creativity has not disappeared – on the contrary. As a consequence of integration, I have a greater number of skills at my disposal, I don't have such frequent gaps in my memory, I can look at the world from a broader perspective, and doing daily chores doesn't tire me excessively. I have the energy to mother my children. On the other hand, I'm conscious of the really sad things in my life and I have to work on them, which, combined with the routines of family life, is exhausting. I've noticed that I'm irritable and lose my temper easily. I have to learn to control myself and re-enter the world of adults. I'm learning to be more patient with myself. As my self-esteem grows, I realise that I also have to redefine my relationships with people. There are times when I need to make painful decisions. The basis of some of my social relationships is so healthy that it is possible to grow together and define things anew, but some relationships come to an end.

Empowering Photography enabled me to view my photos from a new perspective. Suddenly it dawned on me that I actually shone! I've always shone! I've been worth all the caring and love, just like all the lovely children in this world. I realised that though my own mother was, because of being so broken herself, unable to look at me with love, there have also been people who have seen me. Who have hugged, nurtured and loved me. I have been cute and sensitive. Bright and creative.
Glad and wild.
And above all, a survivor made of sterner stuff.

With integration, my "illnesses" have also disappeared.

At the beginning, my therapeutic journey was a real tumult both inwardly and outwardly. For a long time, the outward world felt unsafe to me. I've never been diagnosed with psychosis, but I'm pretty sure that I have occasionally been in a state very similar to psychosis. I've fled from the ghosts of my past in the middle of the night, hiding from the people who have tried to help me. I've imagined that I am having a conversation with my therapist on the phone, though in fact I've been in an almost catatonic state. Despite all my weird behaviour, I've never been admitted to hospital or prescribed medication. Fortunately.

MEDICATION

I was offered medication for the first time when I had a massive panic attack as a teenager in the parking lot of my workplace. I collapsed totally and barely managed to drag myself to my mother's workplace, which was in the neighbourhood. She rushed me to an adolescent psychiatrist's office and left me there. I wanted to get out of there as quickly as possible, and though the psychologist and I should have talked about me, we ended up discussing how she was coping with the tough work. I left there with a prescription for antidepressants, but I don't think I ever even bought them. No-one suggested that I should go to therapy.

I've always had a negative attitude towards antidepressants, though I haven't been so strict about using intoxicants. I guess it's partly because I've seen what strong psychopharmaceutical medication does to a person, as one of my two older brothers was condemned to institutional care as a psychosis patient already in his early teens. Ever since then, he's been heavily medicated and has lived with an incorrect diagnosis. He has now suffered because of this for almost forty years. His schizophrenia diagnosis has occasionally been questioned, and some things have strongly suggested that he may actually have had a trauma-induced psychosis, but he's been on strong medication for so long that he's been exposed to neurological changes. As a teenager, every now and then I was threatened with different kinds of institutions if I didn't behave the way my parents wanted. The idea of sharing my brother's fate scared me to death.

When I started going to therapy and had it roughest, I tried mild anti-depressants. They may have toned down my anxiety, but I didn't like the way I felt. I suffered from severe insomnia, for which I was prescribed both sleep-inducing drugs and strong sleeping pills. They didn't help me fall asleep. On the worst nights, I might take far too many of the strong pills and end up just being nauseous though the dosage could have killed me. I preferred to medicate my anxiety and sleeplessness with alcohol. With a hangover, it was totally quiet in my head, and I could rest. Later, I've been given premedication, for example at the dentist's, with the same result. Though I've swallowed a huge dosage, the medicine has not helped at all. As if I hadn't even taken the pills. But after the operation I sometimes sleep around the clock at home.

Once – when I was much younger – I had a surgical operation but woke up despite being under anaesthesia.

I feel that my negative attitude towards medication has, in the end, been good for me. I do believe that medicines can provide beneficial, temporary support for psychotherapy, but they are not the way to heal traumas. Medicine dulls the symptoms, such as depression, anxiety, self-destruction or insomnia. Unfortunately, they also make many other things feel duller. I feel it would be absurd to believe that medicine could make someone recover from a trauma-related dissociative disorder. Something that has evolved in relationships with people over several years can't be healed with pills. For my dissociative disorder, therapy has been the only medicine that has worked.

As my experience of therapy has been so long, I've often had to defend going to therapy even to the people who are closest to me. It's difficult to describe the therapy process and the relationship with the therapist to someone who has no experience of them. I'm often asked whether it is, after all, healthy and beneficial to tear open the old wounds and wallow in the past. This is exactly what good trauma therapy is not about! If you don't want to, you don't need to ever face all your painful memories. Therapy aims at learning to build a sense of security and cooperation inside you. If you constantly rushed to face traumatic memories, the re-

sult would be something totally different. Thus, my therapist and I have preferred to slow down when faced with memories and concentrate instead on feeling and listening to what is going on inside me. But this has required a great deal of training. There have been moments when I haven't been able to slow down – and the strong bodily memories have resurfaced. I thank myself for having the persistence to continue going to therapy despite the difficulties I've run into. I'm sure my own behaviour has also made people around me oppose and wonder about the therapy. The saying "Things will get worse before they start getting better" is definitely true in my case.

It's exciting to look back to the very beginning and see how my mind has reached the point where it is now. At first I didn't know about "us"; I didn't even believe that a personality could be split. Then I was scared to death that part of me would be taken away if I began to integrate. I didn't even really believe that you could recover from the kind of experience I had had. The word "integration" sounded like a term from science fiction. But here I am now, almost as one. I'm a living example of the fact that you can recover from anything and that a split personality can again become coherent, one personality. Or whatever is enough for each of us. Perhaps for someone it's enough to have the inner parts gather together at one negotiation table. It's up to each one to define for ourselves what "sufficient integration" means.

But there's one thing I know for sure: trauma therapy is the only medicine that works.

I have often looked for an answer to the question "How did I make it?" During this book project, I went through my old archives where I had stored piles of letters, writings, pictures and diaries. I understood that creative expression has been one of the most important ways of processing unbearably difficult issues in my life. I have used writing and art for making visible my experiences and my not being well. What I have created would not have been greeted with acceptance in my young days. My creations have caused the same kind of uneasy silence in my family and friends as photos from my childhood. Though they convey many agonising feelings, they deserve to be looked at with love and compassion. They deserve their place as a visible and accepted part of me and my life.

DYSLEXIA OR A DIFFERENT WAY OF THINKING?

During the first nine years of school, I was an average pupil, though it was difficult for me to study for tests and get my homework done. Listening during the lessons and paying attention to visual material was enough. This was, however, not enough in upper secondary school, so I quickly got behind with my schoolwork. Especially languages and math have always caused me a great deal of anxiety. I did, however, learn languages quickly outside the classroom, and I've done well in sales even though we often have to deal with figures.

When we lived abroad when I was a child, I socialised with an English family living next door, and it took me just a few weeks to learn to communicate in English. If my mother and I didn't want my father to understand us, we used English. That was the period when the first parts of my personality that communicate in English were created. Their task inside me was to work as a bridge and a referee between my different parts. Later, they have got me help in situations where I wasn't able to get it any other way. For example, sometimes when I haven't been able to call or send an SMS in Finnish, I've been able to do it in English.

Thus, I can communicate well orally, but grammar has always been torture to me no matter what the language is. I've always wanted to learn new things, though other people have often had doubts about this. The parts of my personality vary so much in age that the traditional teaching methods have never worked for me. For example, there are parts of my personality that are so young that they can't read yet. The same applies even more strongly to math. I still have to use a calculator even when I'm adding or subtracting just two figures. Fortunately, technology has made the use of calculators and other devices easy.

Not being able to do math has always been a source of shame and anxiety for me. My family has made fun of me because of this. I still get scornful comments concerning this ineptitude from family members, and it can be used as a weapon against me. It's difficult for me to think about things in the form of sentences, figures or written formulas.

I seem to remember that I barely managed to pass the math course in sixth grade. In lower secondary school, we were divided into three

Artwork by Carita

groups according to our skill. I was in the "worst" group. And was I ever lucky, because the teacher who taught the group was just phenomenal! For the first time, I met a teacher who could teach this incomprehensible subject to me – and I learned! Her way of teaching was very visual, and she knew the subject so well that she could approach it from many angles. Albert Einstein's comment "If you can't explain it to a six-year-old, you don't understand it yourself" applied to the situation really well, for this teacher knew the subject and was able to choose words that were suitable to the age level of the pupil when explaining things.

That's when I realised that the trouble wasn't me: I, too, could learn these seemingly difficult things, if I was taught in a way that suited me. My grade went up, and I was moved to a more advanced group. To my disappointment, everything was completely incomprehensible again. Luckily I was allowed to move back to the earlier group where I could follow the teaching and keep my better grade. Another exciting thing was that my grades in physics and chemistry were above average in lower secondary school. I had the same teacher for these subjects, and her teaching was even more visual and based on practice than in math. I became so interested in these subjects that I built a laboratory at home where I did various experiments. I developed all kinds of theories and presented them to my teacher, and together we assessed whether they could be put into practice. I'm extremely grateful to that teacher for this experience during a period that was otherwise tumultuous and filled with distress for me.

In lower secondary level my homeroom teacher, who was also my English teacher, came one day to talk to me about dyslexia, suggesting that I might have it. At the time, I didn't understand at all what she was talking about and why she thought so. It's a pity that no-one ever took the issue up again, because had the problem been addressed then, my school experiences and my life could have been quite different. Of course, there were more pressing issues in my life at the time: I was also bullied at school and showed many signs of not being well. I often went to see the school nurse, who even sent me to a psychologist at the health centre. I seem to remember I met the psychologist once or twice, but those sessions weren't beneficial for me in any way – on the contrary.

Artwork by Carita

I've never let my "dyslexia" restrict what I do, though I occasionally get comments about it. I struggle especially with compound words
and sentence structures. I try to concentrate on being able to convey
the message of my mind's visual world as vividly as possible in writing.
Sometimes I feel that I succeed in this, though my message may be overshadowed by misspellings.

ART

Art has always been for me a way of communicating things that you are not allowed to talk about. I can also analyse difficult things better through images than writing. I can hide a whole story in one picture. Creating images is something that cuts through the whole of my diverse personality structure. When I work, things and themes often seem to just flow out of me. That's when I'm intensely connected with my subconscious.

I've drawn, painted and done clay modelling since I was a small child. I've been interested in everything that has to do with creativity. My works have been worth more than gold to me, because, in them, I've been able to channel feelings that I shouldn't have had; thus, I've been visible, and I've been able to exist. Even at a very young age, I used to flare up if someone broke my works or treated them disrespectfully. It was too much for me. I could stand almost anything else, but not that. I remember how, in first grade, a classmate accidentally sat on a horse and rider I had modelled, squashing them. I was furious and cried uncontrollably. Tumults of feelings used to give me fever. Modelling with clay or plasticine or drawing was the best medicine against it. When I had finished my piece of art, the fever was gone and the difficult feeling had been relocated in the object I had created.

When I was ten, I occasionally drew screaming skulls and cemeteries in art lessons. At the time, I became familiar with the art of Edvard Munch. His works spoke to something in me. Horror, distress, danger – I still recognise things that he hid visibly in his works. Especially his work The Scream was important to me until I was a teenager.

I'm still amazed that none of the adults in my school ever stopped to ask why my art differed so much from the art made by my classmates. In retrospect, things seem so obvious. When I was fifteen, we painted a self-portrait in art by projecting a silhouette of ourselves on a large paper with the help of our own shadows. Inside the silhouette, each one drew his or her mental world. I was praised for my skill, but the work was never hung very visibly. My work describes, better than a thousand words, the dissociative me that I was in my teens. Even then, no-one

Artwork by Carita

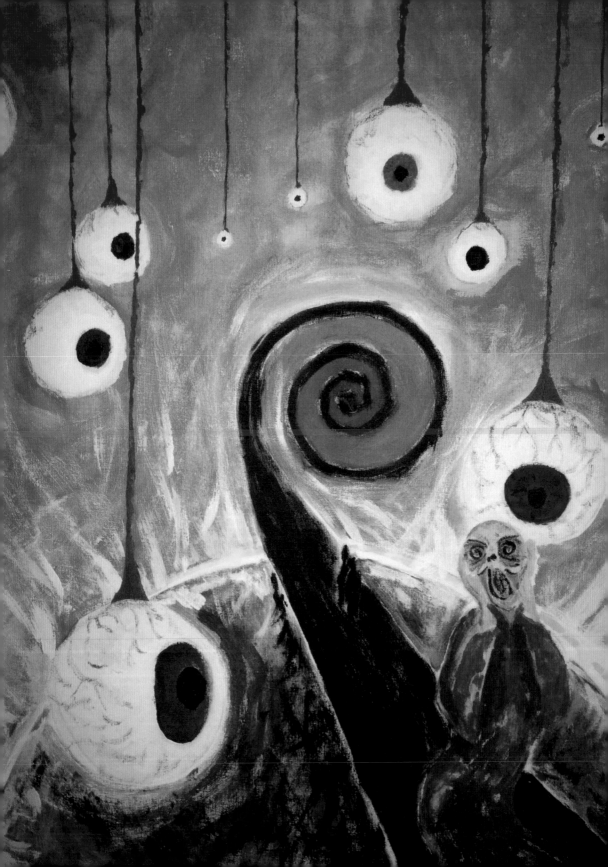

A photo from my bedroom of when I was a teen

wanted to face or see me. When I took the work home and showed it to my mother, she, amused, commented that she saw sexual frustration in it. Touché. They say that it is difficult to recognise dissociation in children. I don't agree with this. Perhaps people don't look for it in the right place, as it is often hidden in a place where it is clearly visible. Or maybe people's own traumas make them blind?

Art has followed me throughout this long journey of mine, and I still continue to tell my stories through it – though more consciously now. Nevertheless, I still notice that I may leave some kind of cues for myself in my works, and sometimes I don't realise their meaning until years later.

Earlier, I used to compare myself to other people, and saw only differences. I've often been isolated and completely alone. In my art exhibitions, I've had the opportunity to meet people who have craved to be seen as much as I have. They've found themselves in my art and stories. People have looked at the things that have been roughest for me, met me and given me love. Acceptance. Through them, I've learned that there are more similarities and connections than differences between me and the world. This way, I've found my way back to a connection with humanity.

Artwork by Carita

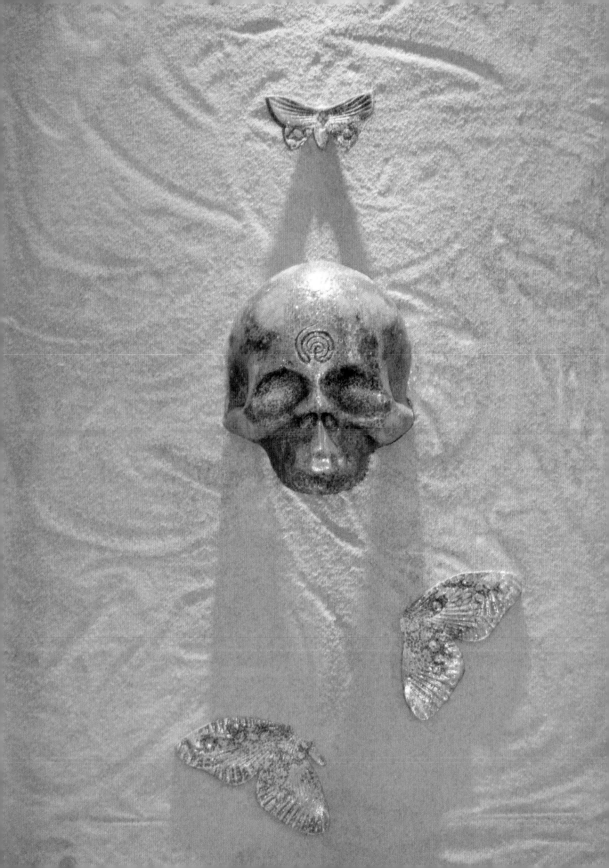

THE DREAM

I had a dream in which I was stuck at the bottom of an enormous, steep dirt pit. It was dark, damp and suffocating. There was danger in the air. I noticed holes in the pit. They were neither very big nor deep. Suddenly it turned pitch black, and I understood that they were open graves. Graves in which children had once been buried, though they were now empty. I got frightened and tried to climb out of the pit, but the soft earth walls gave way every time I took a step. The pit started to grow, and I realised that there were many more graves though they were not open yet. I was afraid and wanted to get away quickly. There were eighty-seven open graves in my dream. I didn't count them, but somehow the figure was given to me – and its significance was stressed. I had to keep the figure in mind. I screamed. I woke up. I felt tired, but there was something special about the dream. That's when I understood how many of us there are in my body.

At night, I'm in contact even with the deepest trauma-induced parts of my personality. It's not unusual even nowadays for me to wake to my own screams at night. The dreams I have on such nights are somehow different from my other, ordinary dreams. They are very gloomy and often repeat certain themes. When they happen, I'm clearly conscious of being in a dream. They used to be terrifying, but that's seldom the case nowadays. They feel interactive and almost like a conversation, though communication happens through scenes, images and feelings instead of words.

I've learned that these dreams have a purpose. A part of me wants to tell me something through them. Understanding this was a great moment. The insight has been liberating for the part of me that uses dreams for communication. It means that I've found a channel that I can listen to and thus tell this part of my self that everything is fine now: "We've survived, and no more evil things will happen." This insight helps me when I go to sleep in the evening. I sometimes get these horrible images in my mind that would have given me a shot of adrenaline earlier, preventing me from falling asleep. Now I can stop to listen to and calm myself. In my mind, I take this part of my personality close to me as if it were my child, lulling it until I fall asleep. It's a wonderful feeling that we can fall asleep in each other's arms, safe.

The real number of the graves in that dirt pit is no longer significant for me: the important thing is to know that there are so many of us and to face my split nature.

RELATIONSHIPS WITH OTHER PEOPLE

An eternal stumbling block? Hopefully not. At least at the level of consciousness, I've also come quite far in this sphere, but I still notice that I often stumble on one thing. My trauma has an impact on everything in my life. It's quite natural that when you are broken in your social relationships – and especially as an infant in your crucial attachment relationships – both your self-image and the picture you have of people in general become distorted.

I feel I've always been adept at being with people, though everything depends, of course, very much on the situation and the depth of the relationship. I've always considered the "real" part of me to be very extroverted, but as I've moved ahead on my journey I've realised that I'm more of an introvert. I prefer to listen to people and to watch, but as I wasn't allowed to be myself as a child I protected myself by creating this exaggerated extroverted part of me. It has felt safe to observe the world from behind this part. This part has also been connected with wearing bright colours and standing out in a group in other ways. This is how I unearth the intentions people have with regard to me. Of course, the picture doesn't always reflect the truth, as I don't let people see me the way I really am.

I make friends easily, but if a friendship begins to grow deeper, I usually start to have trouble with it. I've noticed that I'm frightened especially by people who truly and unselfishly just want time and friendship from me; when friends become closer to me, I no longer know how to be with them. At the moment when I need a friend most I wrap myself up tightly in my loneliness, isolating myself. I don't answer the phone, and once I even cried silently behind the door when a friend of mine, worried, tried to come to see me. This is logical, as the ones who should have taught me to trust people were the ones who broke me.

On the one hand, I run headlong towards people who clearly signal that they don't like me or are not safe for me. I crave their acceptance and use a huge amount of mental energy reflecting on how to behave with them and why they dislike me. On the other hand, I keep them close to me so that I can anticipate their intentions. Although I'm aware of how unhealthy this is, I always seem to end up in this kind of company. This way of operating is familiar and "safe" for me from the period when I was trying to cope with my parents at home as a child and a teenager. This strategy, which is suitable for a "state of war", is exaggerated for the daily life of an adult, but when I was a child it was an essential way of avoiding conflicts and keeping myself safe.

I've often realised that my way of thinking may differ from the way the person with whom I'm discussing something sees the world. I see things as a whole and easily notice connections between different things. I'm sensitive to all kinds of visual communication. I've learned to read the language of non-verbal gestures almost as easily as speech. However, such language often carries a contradiction in it, because the spoken message doesn't correspond to the message given by the body. If I don't know the context, I may misunderstand things, which, in turn, may activate my trauma-induced parts. I've often run into this at a doctor's appointment, for example. Of course, people have many things that they don't want to reveal for various reasons. This means that there's a lot of room for interpretation, and, as I mirror things to my own world of experiences, my presumptions are often somewhat negative. This gives the whole picture a false colour in the end.

As I've progressed with my integration, I've gained more control over the way I interpret situations; this is something that has greatly benefited me. It's now easier for me to understand why communication may be contradictory. This is connected with the things I've learned in therapy. For example, I've learned to mentalise – to understand other people's behaviour in terms of their mental states – and, therefore, put my own reactions into proportion.

Sometimes I meet people whom I can't interpret at all, as if I were blind to their signals. They are the people I fear most. Ironically enough, they are usually also the people who are absolutely altruistic and want nothing from me but friendship. My reaction is connected with a comprehensible inner logic, which is based on the experiences I had of attachment early in life. It is precisely the people who were supposed to take care of me and teach me how to assemble the building blocks of love who broke me worse than anyone else. Love and intimacy set off an alarm in me. Still, I need love and intimacy – something that in itself activates my traumas. What a huge inner contradiction! No wonder I can often be wired and irritated when I'm at home with my husband.

It's easier for me if a person has contradictory motives and thoughts, because I'm used to that, while altruism is strange and frightening to me.

I have a few good friends with whom I find it extremely difficult to be for exactly this reason. They are the very people who have been extremely patient and persistently tried to keep in contact with me for years, though I've been almost impossible to reach.

Once, I felt really tense and nervous when I was with a friend of mine. I had no idea why I was so anxious, but I decided to be brave and tell him that I was anxious because I couldn't read him. He was clearly a bit annoyed and asked why I wanted to read him. I didn't know what to say. I experienced him as a very unsettling person in any case. He seemed to have an incredibly strong inner peace of mind and an understanding of people and the world around him. He once told me about a friend of his who was extremely good at self-defence sports. This friend's life had been stormy. When he was younger he used to practise his moves on stray dogs, for example. I was shocked and overwhelmed by intense hatred. My friend was slightly amused by my disgust, and he went on to say that his friend didn't do it anymore. I decided to ask my friend what he hated. He was a bit surprised again and answered that "hatred" was a big word. He said he didn't hate anything: there were many things he didn't like and he understood that there was unfairness in the world, but he didn't hate anything. I was confused. It took a few years before I could understand that friend.

I sincerely hope that I will one day overcome the hindrances I have in my relationships with people; I hope I will give myself the chance to be with my friends without having my mind in turmoil.

I believe I'm on the right path, because I now know that part of the solution lies in recognising my own value and loving myself. I've learned to feel empathy and love for my inner world, and even take pride in it. I now put my effort into seeing myself, even in terms of appearance, as someone who is beautiful, wonderful and faultless – but in such a way that I also hold on to the things and relationships I've already attained.

Earlier, I would have left everything behind and moved away, fled, in this kind of situation. However, that strategy has always taken me back to the same point. Now I've decided to try something new, and I'm doing the opposite of what my inner voice tells me to do: I don't flee. The method seems to work.

I was very young when I sensed that my parents didn't enjoy my company. They were distant and wanted to have a great deal of time for themselves in the evenings. They didn't listen to me or find what I told them interesting; they were irritated. They usually drank a few bottles of wine every night. This has been the case as long as I can remember. This lack of attention to me is also an issue I need to work consciously on as a parent every day now. Ignoring the child can't be compared to explosive violence directly, but, of course, it's equally damaging to a child's development.

As for couple relationships, I just want to say that "birds of a feather flock together". I've been in both violent and good relationships. However, they've had one thing in common: they've all spoken to my traumas in some way. I've been dominated but I've also been the one who dominates. We never start relationships coincidentally.

I'm married to a nice, kind man. When we met, we threw ourselves into sharing our lives at full throttle. We've achieved a great deal together, but it hasn't been easy. My husband also has a difficult family history. Not the kind I have, but he has also experienced damaging things. When we met, we could understand each other incredibly well. However, as our lives have unrolled and we've grown, each at our own pace, we've often come to a situation in which we've had to look for external help and seriously reflect on our common future. It seems that we easily bring out the worst sides of each other, though we know that we're both good people. So being together requires us to work continuously. Each of us on our own, and together.

When I started going to therapy I cut all contact with my parents. It was traumatic, though, at some level, I understood that they were not safe for me. I grieved their "death" for years, though they were alive and living just a few hundred kilometres away. I still had siblings and the nurturing family of my older brother, but the life-long dividing impact of traumatisation had created a huge chasm between us. We were together but still distant, each an orphan living in his or her own world. It's unbelievable that it took so long until I could sit down with my brothers to discuss our experiences together and mark them on a timeline; this happened just a few years ago. It was difficult, but also a relief. After all, we weren't alone with our thoughts and experiences – this became quite concrete when we talked.

I've been without a community for a long time – a hard thing for a gregarious animal. I'm sure it's one of the reasons why I misread human relationships. I rely too much on my not-so-close friends – and am disappointed over and over. On the other hand, I don't know how to welcome deeper friendship from those who want to give it to me.

IRA

An always alert gatekeeper, my gentle teacher.

Dogs have been an important part of my life ever since I was born. They've been a source of security and companionship, but my relationship to them has also been slightly ambiguous. Probably, the animals of my life have taught me, above all, how to be more human.

When I was small, we had a Rottweiler bitch which was very protective of me. At the age of four, I went wandering in the forest by our cabin, with our dog following me. She stayed near me all the time and made me feel at ease. I remember being happy about it: wolves wouldn't dare to eat me, because Ira was with me. Ira's name was also the first word I uttered when I learned to say the letter R. Ira fulfilled a special purpose: she brought security to my life. There have been several significant dogs in my life, and they've all imprinted their paw trace on me. However, Rottweilers have always had a special place in my heart.

As a child, I often wondered why our dogs were so angry towards people they didn't know. I couldn't understand this until I became an adult and had gone through a total personal failure. My father was violently cruel towards our dogs, and we never trained them through positive reinforcement: if the dog didn't obey, it was given a brutal beating. I was taught that dogs were controlled by showing who's in charge.

When I came of age, I got myself a Rottweiler puppy. Surprisingly, I called her Ira. Ira followed me out into the world, and we grew up together. She never abandoned me, and, in a tight spot, she always defended me. Ira was my dearest family member, and I'm happy that she got to see and smell my first child before dying.

In her life, Ira taught and guided me in invaluable ways, but she gave me her most important lesson when she died. For a long time, I had looked for the reasons for evil outside myself, but, at death, Ira turned the mirror towards me.

In terms of Rottweiler years, Ira was getting quite old – she was even living on borrowed time. Still, I was blind to her deteriorating health. Our child was just a baby, and I was going through a crisis of motherhood. One evening, I pretended not to notice anything when we went for a walk and Ira slowly slogged behind. At home, Ira whined and yelped – something that irritated me. The baby was crying, and I also needed to go shopping. I flew into a rage.

When I came back from the shop, Ira was still lying where I had left her. I saw right away that she was in bad shape. I took the baby to the neighbour's and started to drive to the veterinarian who was on duty. I knew it would not end well. The veterinarian confirmed my gut feeling. A big tumour in Ira's spleen had torn and was bleeding uncontrollably. Ira passed away on my lap.

I felt as if a spear had been thrust through my mind, and all the parts of my personality were screaming at the same time. In all its gruesomeness, this was the first experience that all my parts clearly shared. As if awareness of what had happened found its way to each part's consciousness through the hole that grief pierced through my mind. In addition to my sorrow, I now also had to face my own evilness.

I've been comforted by saying that there really wasn't anything to be done for Ira at that point and that the tumour must have bled for days before that evening. But this doesn't change the fact that I behaved violently towards Ira before going grocery shopping with my child. Instead of hearing my most cherished companion's request for help and giving her a safe, dignified end, she had to go through fear, pain and suffering. Because of me.

Artwork by Carita

Ira gave me the most important lesson I've ever had, opening a door to a new understanding. Because of her sacrifice, my children have been saved from similar suffering.

FURY LIVES IN MY STOMACH

The parts of me that "live in my stomach" have recently risen into the fringes of my awareness. I've avoided them for a long time, because they carry my slimiest experiences and the troubled feelings connected with them. They contain rages of different levels and types. They bring up self-punishment and thoughts of self-destruction. Intense disgust with myself. They are parts that imitate the one who mistreated me.

I'd like to tell more about these parts as I know that they've also been important for my survival and played a crucial role in the progress I've made in integration, but since our cooperation with these parts is just at the beginning, I can't do it very lucidly.

Sometimes it feels as if there is a big numb hole in my stomach. When I look through it, I see darkness that is blacker than black. I see fire and smoke. Don't come here! Don't touch me!

This part of my personality is activated by exercise and especially abdominal workouts. In addition to intense hatred and anxiety, training may give me fever and a headache. Thus physical activity is a difficult thing for me, though I'd like to take better care of myself physically. I keep eating too much, because my stomach doesn't tell me I'm full. I remember punishing myself often with food when I was a teen-ager. I either gulped down huge portions or refrained from eating for long periods. I also did, compulsively, an enormous number of abdominal exercises in the evenings. I remember wondering why I didn't feel any pain despite my rigorous stomach workouts. It must have been a consequence of this numbness.

Artwork by Carita

EASIER TO BREATHE IN THE COUNTRYSIDE

Moving so often in childhood has made me feel every few years that I have to move to a new place. That I have to start over. For a long time, the thought of moving to the countryside felt like a dream that would never be realised – until, one day, it came true. When we moved, I thought it would take at least a year for me to really settle in my new home. But no. Very soon, I felt truly at home for the first time in my life.

Before we moved, I did a lot of work with my insecure parts. In my mind, I placed objects that were important for my various parts in the new home and also verbalised my emotional world to my husband so that he'd be able to take my needs into consideration.

Our new home has an open view in all directions. Nature is nearby and there is a lot of room. Compared with the city or a population centre, there are clearly fewer triggers that make my traumatising experiences resurface. All these factors enable me to feel that I've come home, and, thanks to therapy, I can recognise these factors.

When we moved to the countryside, I was able to realise my dream of raising chickens. We hadn't even started building the chicken house when I was already driving home with the backseat of our Twingo full of cackling transport boxes. I called my husband and said that we had to get down to business. Unexpectedly, the chickens took my view of the world to a completely new level. I hardly knew anything about hens before getting some. Surprisingly, chickens have a rich emotional and mental life. They are very social, gregarious animals. I see that they have many similarities with people. They have close relationships. They mourn if they lose their companion. They can be traumatised and get depressed. They teach important survival skills to their offspring.

My chickens have inspired me to reflect more on the world around me and on how we humans see our position in it. I've found my way back to being part of a cycle, and this has given me a feeling of having influence. I can grow some of my food myself. I can teach my children how to lead a good life in the world. I have the right to exist.

Chickens have proved to be especially effective therapeutical animals for me, possibly partly because I never had any contact with the species

Artwork by Carita

during my period of traumatisation. Thus, I can be with them freely: they never remind me of my past. This has helped me understand that though dogs have been so important for me, they remind me of my traumatic period. This is a useful insight now that I'm learning to replace harmful ways of operating with new ones.

I've always had a special relationship with animals. This may largely be a result of the fact that I've been mistreated by humans. I've been dehumanised – even to the extent that I prefer to identify with something else than the representatives of my own species. I'm sure the sense of security that I felt as a child in the company of our dogs has also contributed to this.

I often found animals on my way back from school and took them home. Thus, I've had a wide spectrum of pets in my life. I've always been able to be my true self in the company of animals: being with them has been uncomplicated. Recently, I've admitted that I've tried to compensate for the deep loneliness I've always felt through my numerous pets. Whenever I face troubled feelings I quickly start planning to expand my animal flock. With increased awareness and progress in my integration, this need has begun to wane. I'm gradually returning to the world of people. It's hard. Almost as if I were learning to walk anew, which, in itself, is funny since I've always been socially adept. However, I now try to be with people as the honest me, as one whole being, without resorting to my protective mechanisms; I try to be simultaneously a visible and a conscious being, for the first time.

I BECAME A MOTHER

My first delivery was traumatic although I thought I had prepared myself well for it. But perhaps I didn't know how to be demanding enough. I lacked a human safety net, and I had had neither cross-generational mentoring nor the guidance I would have needed – something that our society's birth-giving machinery could not provide. I could verbalise my needs well, but that didn't mean I was being heard. I had, at that point, gone to therapy for several years, but, still, the cooperation between the various parts of me wasn't yet strong enough. As a result of many inner factors and the bad care provided to me, the only positive thing I can say about giving birth to one's first child is that my child and I survived the ordeal. The ante-natal care wasn't any better. I can honestly say that if I hadn't had a good therapy relationship and a small peer group of mothers who had given birth to their first child, I, and very probably my child, wouldn't be alive now.

Becoming a mother was a real hell for me.

Biology is an amazing thing. Though I swore that I'd never consider having another child, four years later I stood in our WC with a positive pregnancy test in my hand. Like my first pregnancy, this second one wasn't, by any standards, easy or without complications, but it was still very different and, on the whole, a wonderful healing experience. But I had to work hard to achieve that!

Fortunately, I met a lovely, experienced nurse who worked at a maternity clinic and who had the courage to believe that I was the best expert on myself. She also knew how to make me trust my womanhood – and was honest with me. She directed me to discuss things with midwives who were skilled enough to believe in my experiences and what I told them. They didn't force me into the mould provided by the system. My needs were met flexibly, and I felt that the professionals treating me put as much effort into helping me as I put into preparing myself for giving birth. The situation was also different in another way: I now knew how to require things and didn't stop demanding until I was completely convinced that my message had been received.

I dared to demand things and be reasonably selfish at home, too. I listened to my body and my inner world. In this period, I concluded many inner peace and cooperation agreements. We decided that my inner adults would deal with the matters connected with the delivery and my inner children would move into their refuges during that period.

One concrete thing that I achieved was making delivery clothes. They consisted of a wraparound tunic and trousers in which I could give birth, if needed. I designed features that were rooted in the earth. At the same time when I was sewing the clothes, I also, in my mind, made them into protective armour for some of the parts of my personality. And though I actually got rid of all my clothes during the delivery, they had already fulfilled their prime purpose at that point.

I was accompanied in the childbirth by my husband and a friend, our doula. Her attendance and support was invaluable for both me and my husband. She was a professional midwife, so we trusted both her friendship and her skill. She did a great job working as an interpreter between us and the official midwife and the doctors that treated me.

We were allowed to go home quite soon after the delivery. However, the short time that we stayed as a family on the maternity ward was a warm, secure experience. We were well taken care of and were all allowed to stay in a family room. When we came for a check-up, we were met by a midwife whom I had never seen. Nevertheless, I could read from her affection that the whole team of the maternity ward had prepared themselves to meet us; everyone truly wanted things to turn out well. And that's what happened. For the first time in my life (apart from therapy sessions), I was treated as a human being and my experience was considered valuable.

This has had an enormous impact on how I've been able to manage in the paramount task of my life: being a mother. It has also opened up a whole new world for me on my way to integration.

TWO OVERLAPPING TIMES
Silhouettes from the past

I'm having a session with my therapist and, at the same time, I'm sitting in my room. I'm simultaneously thirty-three and thirteen. I see the familiar, safe objects and things in my therapist's office. I see the wooden walls and the posters that decorate them in my small room. I hear the screech of trams and someone's hurried steps on the street. It's totally quiet. I wait. We wait. We look at our therapist through the same eyes. We hear through the same ears. We answer through the same mouth. Two times at the same time. I can now leave one of them behind. I rise from my bed and climb the stairs to the upper floor. Just like so infinitely many times before. I do it now knowing that the door will open up to the present.

From double consciousness to integration.

THE MEANING OF THIS WRITING PROCESS AND PEER SUPPORT

During my long therapeutic journey, I've been able to create a sense of security in me, which, in turn, has enabled inner cooperation between the different parts of my personality. Gradually and one at a time, my parts have become more aware of the present. However, in the past half year, I've progressed in great leaps in integration and in becoming aware and more coherent. There's one simple reason for that: the empowerment and sense of belonging that the peer group that has formed around this book project has given me. This group has been the last missing part.

Of course, I've read, heard and even watched videos about other people who struggle with dissociative disorder in the course of my therapy, but you can't compare it with the experience of meeting another human being, alive and breathing, in an interactive situation. Suddenly, I was no longer physically alone. Suddenly, I actually had a community around me! I was fully allowed to be myself.

This experience gave me strength and courage to come out with my story. Fully as the person I am. I'm not ashamed even if social situations have felt like learning to walk again. Partly because I know that I'm not alone with this experience, either. The more I've dared to verbalise my experiences in ordinary, daily interactions with people, the more clearly I realise that, despite my pain, I may actually not be so very different.

Verbalising and putting my story and experiences in writing has changed my life in a profound way. I remember how my therapist suggested – at the beginning of therapy – that I might want to write stories about my life. It felt like a wonderful idea, but every time I stared at the empty page, my mind froze up completely. I had only been able to deal with my stories through images and speech. However, now I've finally been able to write about them.

The process of writing constantly offers me new inner and external insights. However, it's not a continuous gush of relief: it's also exhausting. When I started writing, I was really enthusiastic and could produce a surprising amount of text. But with the deadline approaching, writing began to feel like a heavy load. I've run into the same feeling every now and then during therapy if I've tried to "force" my way through the defences of my mind. My inner consensus begins to waver, and some of my insecure parts push forward. At the moment, this is manifested as headaches and nosebleeds. Another reason that writing is challenging and slow is that I have, in me, several opinions about and experiences of almost everything. I write paragraphs that are as short as possible, because if I stop writing and return to the text later, it's hard for me to get connected with what I was writing earlier.

Such a way of writing is a new, invaluable skill for me, and I'm sure I will continue writing throughout my life. Though with no deadlines from now on.

FINALLY...

I wrote the following words four months after I met the incredibly brave, intelligent, wise and talented members of our peer group for the first time:

I managed to visit the bottom of my mind's well. It was terribly dark there. A small, frightened child was sitting there alone. I took her on my lap and hugged her. I held her tightly and gently, but swore at the cruel world at the same time. I cried. I write in metaphors about what I found. There's no need to repeat everything aloud. I understood and saw that there was an extremely good reason why my mind broke into pieces.

I stepped out of the dark with the child in my arms. I told her that we had made it. I carry her with me like a child of my own. I'm good to her, I love her. I'm patient and gentle. I give her security and protection. I teach and guide. In return, she gave me myself.

Thus, I reached an important goal on my long and rocky way. It was a bleak moment. However, strength forced its way through the sorrow and the hatred. The shame was gone. I was determined to stand proudly in front of my life. I also felt happy.

My victory seems coarse and bittersweet, but I am free. Twelve years of therapy has provided me with the tools and the energy to build a sense of security. To reassemble myself piece by piece. But I wouldn't have found the key to the final door without other people. Without my peers: the kindred spirits who have led me back to people.

They've made me feel safe, they've accepted and understood me. Despite my wounds, I've felt useful. I haven't needed to hide or be ashamed. I've been given strength, and I've had the chance to offer it as well. I've got a mission and my life has meaning.

Today, I stand here in front of you strong enough
to carry the load of my mind.

I have a community.
I have a mission.
I'm meaningful.
I'm of great value.

So are you.

You can survive anything.
I promise.

With love,
Carita Kilpinen
Survivor

#my body remembers

SEIJA

I'm a woman in my 50s and a mother. I work in various visual professions, and, at my core, I'm an artist. I've often lived abroad, and I'm extremely committed to the things I want to realise in life.

However, there's one disturbing thing in my life: I have a dissociative disorder, and coping with it takes a hell of a lot of energy. I was thirty-one and alone at home when a series of memories suddenly surfaced in my consciousness: I'd been sexually abused for years.

The thought of incest felt strange. Why did these filmstrips show themselves to me now when I'd just begun a relationship with a man for the first time in my life?

For a few days, I wrote and drew, and eventually a kind of picture of what had happened emerged on the paper: between the ages of five and twelve, at home and in the sauna. Finally, I told my family about my suspicions, causing a range of reactions. One sister doubted and refused to believe me; the other one admitted that similar things had happened to her but didn't want to talk about it because she'd decided to leave everything behind. Our mother was already dead, and our father denied everything with his hand on the Bible. Ill at ease, our other relatives would change the subject. My partner supported me, writing angry letters to my father.

I was a strange, bullied child, and I liked to isolate myself as a teenager. Talking about incest made me feel even more disconnected now as an adult, launching me for good in an orbit of my own. I'd just got a new identity as a victim of abuse. How was I to live with it?

As an adolescent, I was very anarchistic – though creative – living outside society and travelling from one country to another. Now, I was back in my native country, and all of a sudden my mind decided to tell me the truth – which mainly led to more confusion.

It would have been easy to redeem this new truth as an all-embracing evidence and explanation for why I'd been so emotionless, disconnected, self-destructive and angry. But who in me would be able to redeem this truth? The me who received the information but had no memory of such things happening? Or the little girl who experienced all this but grew up to be an obedient, withdrawn schoolgirl and a distressed adolescent? How would that girl be able to tell her story now, if she'd once been silenced, frightened so that even the thought of prison felt safer and more attractive to her than that of home and family?

At that point I realised perhaps more clearly than ever that I wasn't getting anywhere with myself. This state of being stuck had gone on since childhood and would continue until death, as there was no liberating way out for me. Later, I learned that such a feeling of being stuck is called "dissociative disorder". It's a condition where the different parts of

Artwork by Seija

So who am I?
Why am I here?
Where am I going?
Just do what you have to do.
Yeah, that sounds nice.
Fuck, do you really think so?
That is a disaster!
But I told you, you should wait! STOP!!!
Just ignore that.

the mind tell different stories about reality, all at the same time.

ABUSE

"You must re-experience the old tragedies consciously, in new contexts, and complete your grief work. Give up the illusion of a happy childhood, and you will feel encouraged. As a result, the intensive and psychotic emotional life of your childhood will become less strange and threatening. You will no longer need to hide it behind illusions, illusions that form a prison around you.

The more unrealistic the feelings aroused by the false, still unknown part of me are, and the smaller the role they play in the present reality, the more they reflect past situations. The memories of these situations have not yet awakened. In me, there's an undiscovered child who tries to resist all this. She creates new ideals to strive for in life, and tries to put them into practice. This way of functioning is not based on real needs and authentic feelings. I give up once again and deny my real self in order to be accepted."

I wrote this intuitively after the filmstrips on incest became active in my head. I didn't yet understand how vast the issue was.

My childhood was a serious, grim and oppressive time. We seldom laughed or joked at home. We weren't even allowed to listen to music, except for the kind of music my father wanted to hear – and when he wanted to hear it. We hardly ever had any guests. I don't remember any discussions. We always sat quietly at meals.

Our father also determined how we should put the shoes in the shoe rack or the handset on the telephone. If you didn't do it the way he wanted, you lost part of your weekly pocket money. If you protested, you were spanked – that is, given a birching with a branch that hung on the wall in the bathroom. It was used to slit your thighs open. After a spanking, we'd go to the playground hand in hand.

My father was a primary school teacher and my mother a housewife/nanny. My father admired Hitler and would have joined the SS if only they had accepted him. My mother was physically seriously ill, and her

160

condition degenerated during my childhood; because of her illness, she treated me with emotional indifference. She always had the meals ready for my father and me when we got home from school. When I was small, I sometimes sat at the back of the class, listening to my father teach. He demanded that every girl wear her hair either in a ponytail or braids. I always had to do that – or I'd look like a whore.

My first memories of sexual abuse go back to the age of five. Father comes to me, smiling. I smile back. Father is nice. He lifts my skirt and touches me. I have many such memories, and, little by little, they start to contain other violence, too. At the age of twelve I collapse in some way. There are mazes all around, and I fall to the bottom of a deep chasm. Why doesn't anyone help me? Then I feel that I'm soaring. I come to a lovely heaven where angels take care of me in a blooming meadow. I'm in the air, wrapped in cellophane and nursed by laser rainbow light.

After this experience, I metaphorically tread my path in life carrying a loose penis. It's wrapped in cling film and cloth and I take it every-where. I realise that, finally, my father is no longer a part of me. I wrap more cloth around the penis. I feel triumphant, but don't know who I am. I can't talk about what's happened, because I must protect my father.

This is what I remember about my childhood. I have two older sisters, who had already moved out by this time. They tried to stay in contact with us at home, but, based on the letters I wrote to them, I didn't get any answers to my questions on why I could not be me. One sister ignored my direct questions though she was also a victim of incest, and the other one pushed her own ideology that people are basically good.

My mother came from a family of rune-singers in Russian Karelia. Still, I can't recall her ever singing a song for me. She looks cheerful in photographs, and I suppose I got some sense of security from the fact that she was always at home, baking cinnamon buns and physically available for me. I grew up together with my niece, and we supported each other as much as possible. We felt that no one else in the fami-ly could understand us in the slightest. I never met my grandparents, and the other relatives didn't have any contact with us. No one liked my father. I suppose the sense of security I felt in childhood was strong enough to keep me from killing myself, though I wanted to.

SHAME

I remember that I was ashamed of everything in me, even my breathing, as early as primary school. This shame seemed to whisper the words "You should not live, you have no right to live". The shame led to an increasing number of failures, which just strengthened my sense of being an outsider. I didn't know how to be me, and my self-esteem was extremely low. I recall that, in secondary school, I sought refuge in the homes of other children, to experience some joy through someone else's family.

In adolescence, I tried to be active in the parish, Girl Guides and the conservation movement. In upper secondary school, my anxiety was at its highest point, and I spent many lessons hiding in the cellar of the school. My sister decided to send me to the USA as an exchange student so that I'd focus on something else. I smiled politely for the whole year, but felt like a complete outsider in every family. Nevertheless, I got to see California and in many ways felt at home in the country in general.

The day after I graduated from school in Finland I set out hitchhiking abroad. My aim was to go far enough to get rid of my family. My mother died soon after my departure, and I finally felt free. I didn't mourn for my mother. I didn't deal with my grief until recently.

My father lived much longer, but we never got close to one another. At some point after he fell seriously ill, I began to keep in touch with him, trying to unravel the secret. He denied everything and took the secret with him to the grave. I could never hate him: instead I saw his helpless and lonely side. I recall how I mailed a photograph to him when I was living abroad during my adolescence, writing on it: "Do you accept me now?" In the photograph, I was dressed in a Nazi officer's uniform. But more than anything else, I longed for my father to accept me as myself, the way I was.

I believe that most of my father's own traumas were war traumas, as he fought in the war for five years. Until just a few years ago, I didn't understand how guilty he probably felt about serving as a commander in the war. This guilt was passed on to me. I'm a leader by nature, like my father, but whenever I've tried to assume this role, I've been overwhelmed by deep horror and the feeling that if I make decisions for other people, something terrible will happen.

During one of the projects I have launched I went down with severe pneumonia just a day before the field phase of the project began. I didn't realise I was sick though my temperature was 40.5 degrees. I went out in the field in my dissociated state, because I wanted to be active and work on this positive and important family project. Of course, I ended up being taken to hospital by ambulance.

Shame may be the biggest and deepest problem I've had to face in my life. Everything about me is wrong, destroyed, not permitted, and evil, evil, evil. No one and nothing in me can protest this: it's just the way it is. It's difficult to live with shame, so the feeling has to be compensated for in some way.

GOOD ME – BAD ME

When abroad, I had a series of good me – bad me periods. The transitions from one to the other were dramatic and usually took place within a single day, with a new part of my personality guiding my life. The transition felt as if a land roller had driven over me. I could only give in, step aside. As if my brain had been shut off and my body had gone through a transformation.

Wanting to learn about organic cultivation through practice, I tried to find ecological communes out there in the world when I was young. However, it was hard for me to feel secure in communes, as I never knew what was normal behaviour and what wasn't. Sometimes there was a crazy Eco-Nazi dictating when I could take a shower or go for a walk by myself, and sometimes I was accused of selfishness because I couldn't be sociable enough. Eventually, I withdrew to the Mediterranean coast to live alone, to write and draw. I earned money any way I could, for example, by painting street art.

I was only fifteen when I began to have visions of the future; one of them concerned ecological villages. At that point, there was no Green movement or internet, so I left Finland to look for ecological communes

I remember that I was
ashamed of everything in me,
even my breathing, as early as
primary school. This shame
seemed to whisper the words

"You should not live,
you have no right to live"

and ways of living, relying only on my visions. I thought that such communes must exist somewhere, because I'd seen them in my mind. Similarly, I had visions of future health care in the late 1970s, with physicians reading digital information about the patient's body on a big screen – which we're finally starting to do with the help of robots. Partly because of this vision, I've hardly ever wanted to take any medicine. I've always felt that you can, to a great extent, take care of your health by controlling your mind, and that's what I've done.

I have a theory about trauma opening up new dimensions in a human being such as the ability to see the future. Could this be a result of me, as a dissociative person, having to live so much in my own imaginary world? Or could it be the result of the sexual trauma breaking a big hole in my body that takes me to other dimensions? One day, I'll find a scientific explanation for this! Anyway, I've been rescued by the fact that I've trusted my own mind when it comes to visions of this kind. When I was on the move, I could, for example, see a street corner in Manhattan though I'd never been to New York, and then I went there with no plans where to stay or anything else. Things always worked out. When I had a child and started a family and had to give up my spontaneous lifestyle, I seized up. I could no longer grasp things intuitively in advance when I had to live in the settings of a normal home, shop, day care and work. I was totally lost.

One day when I was again hitchhiking across Europe to Finland to earn money by jobbing, a voice in my head told me that I'd had enough of this kind of life: it was time to move on to experience evil. I had no idea what the voice was talking about, but, in just a month, I found myself wearing black leather instead of my old hippie clothes. Soon two new mates of mine and I started an anarchistic women's group that focused on art and sadomasochism. And did so very publicly.

Next, I found myself living in the subcultures of big cities like London and New York. I preferred to live in slums, in warehouses or buildings that were falling apart. I felt they were beautiful. Being disconnected was the best thing I knew, and ignorance was an expression of love. I was fascinated by the diversity of the world and its different cultures.

These cities that pulsed with all that was new in the 1980s were good stages for my inner worlds. We made art, videos and performances, and organised clubs where we danced all night. Life was characterised by self-expression and a form of playfulness. The energy behind the playfulness may have come from emptiness, violence, anxiety and pleasure, but it was still creative. Maybe living and experiencing my strange fantasy world was just the thing that enabled me to stay in my right mind and, despite everything, love and care in my own way. In our global commune, numerous lonely creative souls met and many found a home.

For me, a survivor coming from an insecure home, it seemed like a secure and organised world. Still, my gatekeeper self was constantly on the alert. It watched especially carefully to make sure I didn't mess up my mind with drugs or alcohol, for example. I experimented a bit with both, but I couldn't take the risk of losing control completely. For this, I have to give credit to my dissociative disorder and the mechanism that supports the functioning of my daytime self.

I found myself in the midst of gunfights between gangs and, eventually, outside the law in various ways. Finally, this phase of my life came to an end. One day when I was arrested and taken to pre-trial custody, I heard a voice rising in me, saying that this was enough. The voice forced me down on my knees, and I clearly felt it take over. As a result, I confessed what I had done and was convicted to prison for two years. Fortunately, the sentence was later changed to a conditional one.

This is how I experienced my life at that point. I heard voices and saw my other selves walking by me. I didn't know who I was, but neither did I stop to think about it. In a way, my whole world of experiences, including what I heard and saw in those days, was normal for me, as I could, nevertheless, use my intellect and creativity quite satisfactorily. I studied video production and graphic design and mastered programmes that were still, at the time, quite difficult to use.

I wasn't afraid of anything, and the world didn't feel like a threatening place. In a way, evil didn't even exist for me. I felt I could always see inside people, through their exterior, detecting mostly goodness in a seemingly wicked world. I now understand that if I had brought the existence of evil into my world of experiences, my childhood insecurity would also have burst forth. I would have had to face the fact that I'd

Artwork by Seija

been really frightened as a child, almost fearing for my life. And that I'd experienced the world as completely irrational, probably ever since early childhood.

I also ignored danger because I was so keen to experience positive things such as joy, creativity and adventures and to be appreciated for what I was doing, through shared involvement. The overwhelming shame that lived in me was there all the time, lurking behind every contact and everything I did. I had to leave, disappear, go away and escape from one place to another constantly. I didn't know how to deal with the shame and the anxiety it caused. I needed to make sure that I didn't expose myself to any more unexpected situations where I'd have to be ashamed of myself, because the shame I was carrying was almost killing me. Such an unexpected situation could have been, for example, too close a relationship, the surfacing of my insecurity, or being criticised.

I have no regrets about spending my youth on the fringes of society. I felt alive. I had a relationship and travelled with a person who was extremely important to me. We gave each other strength, though our relationship was not a conventional one. My friend was a both-feet-on-the-ground type – unlike me. I was never afraid of losing her, and our splits were never very tragic. I believe that my nomadic-type life fulfilled my need for both socialising with and avoiding people.

Sexuality was for me the same as creative energy. There were times when I could feel pleasure only through pain. At one point, sex was even the basis for my art. Not until my next good-me phase began and I paused properly did I notice that I couldn't even feel the touch on my skin when I brushed my arm.

What I now know about the brain's ability to change throughout life has freed me from my worry that I might have ruined myself during this phase of life. I don't feel like a criminal. Neither do I consider myself violent, though at one time, no doubt, I might have lifted my hand against anyone who dared to be rude to me. I knew that I would be able to kill, but I thought that I at least recognised the truth about human nature and was not phony. There was a deep-rooted darkness in me, and I was aware of it when it began to surface. I didn't remember anything about those moments, but the traces were always there.

However, there was also a little Seija living in my brain to whom I didn't know how to pay attention at the time. My massive disappointment over my love not being returned as a child had left me alone and driven me to reject the child in me. Not until I was over fifty was I able to identify with the small girl crying on the street who was comforted by her father and lifted up to his shoulders, to a safe place. When I saw this, I felt a deep longing for a secure childhood for the first time. I also know that the little Seija was really frightened when I roamed abroad looking for adventure, and I'm also tending to the wounds of those years now.

In addition, I've begun to grasp how insecure and alone I must have been as an infant and toddler. The world was unstructured, and apparently nothing was explained to me. Did my parents look at me, did they talk to me, did they tell me what was happening and when? Were my basic needs fulfilled, was I nurtured, or was I left crying alone? Emptiness has always been my basic state of mind, with no room for a self or an ego. Lack of nurture leads to attachment disorder. Not until I started undergoing individual therapy did I have a permanent, deep experience of being valuable simply because I am me. This experience may be the most important thing in my life, in addition to having a child and a spouse.

MOTHERHOOD, HOME, FAMILY...

I've been lucky enough to have a wonderful child and a wonderful partner. Already long before they became part of my life I decided to start focusing on empathy and peace. For a while, my way of life consisted of serving others. I helped, served, nursed and listened to people whenever possible. In retrospect, I wish I'd had the sense to focus on myself and face my fears already at that point. Serving other people was, again, a way of shifting the attention away from my real problems. In the end, the attempt to be a good and decent person left my innermost self empty.

I moved into this good-me phase by tearing myself loose from the old me in just a few days: a new person stepped in forcefully, once again.

I withdrew and started to meditate alone, I broke off almost all my old friendships and began to dress in a different way; my old friends seldom recognised me on the street. I got involved in charity work.

I became aware of having been molested just a year before I got pregnant. Therefore, my first years as a mother were the most difficult ones. Sometimes I was so disturbed by the overwhelming traumatic memories that kept surfacing day and night that I took my child to my friend's place and lay alone under the blankets. I was afraid that I might do something bad to my daughter or myself. I also tried to get help from the public health services, but at the time there were no groups for mothers who had been victims of incest.

At the age of six, my daughter asked me riddles: "Mum, what's the future of the heart? And what's the future of human beings, and the sea?" The correct answers were joy, love and life. With such an optimistic child, I was worried that I might damage or discourage her, even ruin her, in some way.

At the practical level, our family life was a mess at first, as I didn't know how to move on from my resurfacing traumatic states in everyday life. We kept moving. At the worst, we stayed in a dirty hostel, paid for by the Social Services Office after we had to destroy all our things as a result of mould problems in our previous home. At that point, my traumatic past was closer than ever and my experiences of being neglected were totally raw.

There were periods when we were so poor that my daughter turned the situation upside-down: "We're different. No one else's mum has just five cents!" I didn't know whether to be proud of her comment or not. Nevertheless, I managed to be a rather sensible mother despite my dissociative mind, the constant pain in my body, the anxiety over my traumatic memories and my inelegant work life. We frequently lived in a commune so that my daughter had different kinds of adults and young people around, as well as the opportunity for a social life even though things were bad for me and my mind was often a mess.

My wise self channelled me into a large number of mental exercises, which I used as the basis for home exercise courses that focused on healing the heart. This is how I earned money to buy food. I also worked as an intuitive seer, as my dissociation helped me to enter other people's minds and interpret their lives. I grabbed a stool and went to give massages to people on the street. Think of all the inner resources you can tap into in periods of extreme need! I want to stress that you can find strength in yourself even if you're really traumatised and struggling with a dissociative disorder and don't even know which of your observations are real and which are not. It may be hard to realise the amount of strength you have, but it's there!

Your strength grows, for example, when you begin to take life and its different situations as a challenge because you're under duress and there are no longer any other alternatives. You begin to look for solutions because you must. You become optimistic almost as if by accident. This creates a whirlwind that picks you up and carries you forward – and you don't have to give in. Dissociation is, of course, linked with falls – really big ones – but you can rise from them! Personally, I have gambled everything, suffered a great deal because of it, and then continued my life. At least half of the time, the suffering has also consisted of pleasure. In almost everything, there's always the other side. Hopefully, my story will encourage other people to tap into their resources.

Going to therapy helped me with being a mother. My daughter is healthy and intelligent and shows no signs of traumatisation. However, she has felt neglected, because I used to dissociate a great deal in her presence. I chose discussion as my method of child rearing, as I didn't know any other way. My child has grown into a young person who's aware of things and good at solving problems. Partly, this is a result of my always being very honest with her and letting her see my emotional sensitivity and the way I've struggled to cope with my traumas in therapy. Maybe the most important thing for me has been not to pass down my traumas to another generation. I've succeeded in breaking the chain, and I really admire myself for this.

I was over forty when this strong vision began to emerge in me: I wanted a whole family and a home. Having been a vagabond and in changing relationships for so long, I didn't even remember at first what family and home actually meant. Once I got the idea, I launched my mission to get a family. It took a few years and living in a few cities until

I finally found the man I had seen in my vision. The three of us made a home. I also seized upon my vision for work, aiming to update my skills in my old vocation in media and start a company. These were the external structures on which I relied when I finally began to go to a professional trauma therapist. I'm still on that road.

CONFUSION

For a long time, it was hard for me to understand the course my life had taken. Why did I choose to live the way I lived? Why did I switch between the different parts the way I did? The story wasn't coherent. Naturally, my therapist had no experience with the kind of life I had led. I sometimes wondered whether I should go to therapy with, for example, a group of ex-convicts in order to have a better opportunity to identify with someone in the thick of my conflicts. Moving along the good-bad axis messes up the mind even without a dissociative disorder. With the disorder, the narrative becomes really complex.

Not until I was able to identify, on a deeper level, the parts in me that had emerged in my childhood and school years did I begin to understand their different needs and the role they had played in my choices. Some of them felt safe when I was leading a criminal and anarchistic life, while others felt safe when I spent my days in our home in a nice neighbourhood. Home as such, as a space, has never been a good solution for me, but the privacy it offers has been good. I still feel anxious about having walls around me, and I'd prefer to sleep in a simple treehouse, under the open sky.

I went to a therapist for the first time long before I had a child. I never went back, but the therapist asked me an important question: "Has it ever occurred to you that your life is not normal?" Well, it hadn't: for example, violence was part of it, at least in my environment. The therapist's words planted a seed that grew in my mind. First, I tried to strip away everything that was not normal in me by engaging in my own consciousness therapy, by meditating, by painting, by writing and by going to various forms of body-orientated therapy. Most of them only made my mind a bigger mess, as all the therapists explained my symptoms in terms of their own world-views. Not many body-orientated therapists know about traumatisation, let alone are able to take it into consideration in their work.

It's frightening how easily you can be stuck with wrong beliefs when you're young. No one stopped to deal with my problems in time. I cannot even imagine how much I must have feared everyday life as a child and how often I must have tried to talk about it without being heard. Suppression, violence, sexual abuse, threats, blackmail and blame became coded in me as different reactions of the body and mind, with cause and effect relationships that seem impossible to decipher as an adult.

Traumatisation and the dissociative disorder are a result of having to protect oneself from a total destruction of the personality, faced with the great irrationality of life. Little by little, the inner protective system begins to resemble inner warfare. The traumatised mind becomes its own enemy and accuser, becoming even crueller than the childhood abuser was in his or her deeds. This happens because the mind can't – and doesn't know how to – face the pain alone, as well as the suffering the evil act has caused. Help is desperately needed!

Below is a poem I wrote at the age of twenty-one when I was living alone in a small village on the coast of Andalusia. I feel it's quite far-sighted.

Am I there now?
a seeker; with a mark on my forehead
of a longing
for what is so distant
restless, steadfast, happy, sad,
I'm pulled forward by a fate that springs
from an inner imperative
I think and think, meditate and almost see
as if in a mirror
feel the lightest breath of air
and the roar of the storm, intense
as omens, marks
they reveal
my path, signs, milestones
I've made progress again
to some extent, a great extent left
still
hurry or dawdle
it's all the same, they both burn
the glow of the fire in me
and finally completely burnt up, exhausted
I've reached what I dreamt of
what I've craved with all my soul...
and I assert:
it was all necessary

Artwork by Seija

I don't want to — and can't — describe the parts in me that were victims of abuse. Most of the time I was gone, dissociated. Sometimes when I'm really confused I want to crawl like a baby. And if I could, I'd hide under the table or the bed, in the furthest corner. There are no words, just immobility and a void around me.

ON THE PARTS OF THE PERSONALITY

A dissociative disorder means experiencing the self as consisting of many parts. Control is the best friend of everyone who suffers from dissociation. Without control and constant checking, the different parts of the personality will throw everything into chaos. You have to keep your face steady and control the movements of your body. This way, the different roles don't surface so easily, and your behaviour and external appearance seem normal. This protocol helps a great deal until you start to work continuously on the parts in order to identify, hear and unite them.

I couldn't recognise the irrational fear and insecurity of my child parts until my therapist provided a mirror for me. The feeling of security has been a new experience for me, and, suddenly, life has got a new face. However, therapy has also maximised my experience of fear and insecurity, as I've become aware of my anxieties and traumas. Dissociation had, of course, made it possible to cover them – indefinitely if needed!

For example, getting up from a chair suddenly or any other natural move from one state to another may be really frightening for the child parts and lead to a switch in personality states. I may be sitting and working at my computer, feeling safe. When I get up, the parts that were unprotected when I was a child are faced with a new situation – always a potential threat for them. I can never know what will happen. At one time, the unpredictable, scary parent might suddenly hit me. He had been nice just a while ago, but was now a punisher. A trivial event like this can result in a switch of parts and turn daily life momentarily into something uncontrollable.

The child parts of my personality have borne the greatest shame. It becomes manifest in varied and strong personality states that have kept resurfacing for years: for example, a desperate girl who stares straight ahead, frozen. The desperate thought that nothing will succeed recurs. The mere presence of change in my life defies the child parts of my personality so that they begin to sabotage the creation of new things by forcing me to pay attention to pain somewhere in my body. Earlier, severe pain from neuralgia made it impossible for me to work – some-

Artwork by Seija

times for days. The warrior part of my personality – which sometimes defends me aggressively – can't stand the part that contains the shame, because it's weak.

Another childhood part of my personality is an invisible, ethereal and distant girl. She feels that there's no room for her. She doesn't know what she looks like, but feels that she is too different. If she could, she'd change everything about herself. She seldom lets me be and constantly sabotages my thinking by causing nausea.

Shame also expresses itself as the feeling that I'm breaking into pieces. As a result of this feeling, I usually leave my body in a way that's almost automatic and start hovering somewhere outside everything. The basic message of the part that leaves the body, like that of many other parts of my personality, is: "I hurt". The girl has been crushed and she's in a stagnant state of mind. She reacts quickly to conflicts. Her response can be triggered by something as simple as having to choose between two things. When this happens, I soon realise that I've been invalidated and feel that there cannot be such a thing as "the self". And since it doesn't exist, it can't choose anything. It doesn't even have a right to exist. I sometimes fall into an even darker state in which this part of my personality wakes me up by telling me that I'm dead. It's the most effective way of invalidating your self, of ending the existence that has no right to be.

This burden of shame is heavy. It consists of deep sorrow that has always cast a shadow on my existence. I've borne the hate and shame of generations. In our family, I've been the bearer of shame, the one to blame for everything. Whenever someone in the family has started his or her own therapy process, I've been partly released from these heavy shackles. Every time, it has made it easier for me to breathe.

I've also discovered a hidden optimistic little girl in me that loves nature. She has a lightness that I've experienced whenever I've lived as a recluse on a mountain or done voluntary work on a flower and herb farm, communicating with plants instead of people. I wish this side of me would grow stronger in my everyday life, among people and in all interactions.

The parts linked with sexual abuse are much harder to deal with. I feel that I've had my father living in my head. I panic whenever his dirty, filthy voice, look or touch goes through me. I start to shout, soundlessly, to myself: go away, go away! I close my eyes to prevent anyone from noticing my lecherous look. I lock my arms so that my fingers won't penetrate any child – even in my mind.

When I'm walking down the street, I sometimes hear my father's voice calling the approaching people dirty, fat or filthy. I guard myself, watching to make sure that I don't send such signals to other people. Even if I don't pay attention to my father's voice, the small child in me hears – and panics, because this voice was the one that always criticised and belittled us. The child part in me induces a bodily reaction: for example, I may lose my hearing or stumble and fall. I don't realise what's happened until I find myself lying on the ground.

I don't want to – and can't – describe the parts in me that were victims of abuse. Most of the time I was gone, dissociated. Sometimes when I'm really confused I want to crawl like a baby. And if I could, I'd hide under the table or the bed, in the furthest corner. There are no words, just immobility and a void around me.

It's sometimes really hard to be a mother, because when I comfort my own child, my inner child may panic. For her, comforting means that something bad may happen soon. A feeling of being threatened emerges in me: something is about to happen and I'd better hide quickly under the bed.

I've had a range of warrior parts, especially aggressive ones, in me. They represent power. You don't want to threaten them, because they'll hit back. They're like my bodyguards, who check and are suspicious about everything at first. They also use some kind of telepathy, trying to protect me and create order in my life.

They're the strength that has allowed me to travel the world almost without fear. Guided by my inner power, I used to go where I wanted and do what I felt like doing. Sometimes I was thrown out of women's toilets because I looked more like a man. A tall person with a shaved head and wearing leather and big boots doesn't have to worry about being threatened.

Part of my strength, hate and intellect has been committed to allowing the parts of my personality to guide me to get whatever I want, by fair means or foul. They've been willing to do anything. Earlier, they also drove me strongly towards getting back at men in every possible way. It took some time before I managed to keep my nose clean, to stay on the right side of the law.

As in all people, there is, of course, both a wise and an observing part in me. These parts are well on their way to becoming integrated into my personality.

But I, the gatekeeper, am the most important figure. I'm the primary controller now. Both hate and power have their own place in me. Nowadays, I recognise my borders, so I also know when they're being crossed. If needed, I can be determined and angry in the right way.

SYMPTOMS ABOUND

"Disso" is a chatty and even playful name for things which are difficult to understand but which will, when not understood, easily stigmatise a person as seriously insane. I might be crazy, but in a positive way. By leaving my body I can get to a refuge where I feel good. Disso has also saved my life. What makes healing difficult is that as soon as I become aware of an emotion, I have to let myself flee to my soft cotton world if dealing with the feeling seems, at that point, too demanding. It's good to understand that I'm processing an agony that I was once unable to face, so I'm all mixed up every now and then! But not insane.

I've regularly defined my relationship to people and places through the pain in my body. How much my body hurts, how sick and dizzy I feel, and how frequently I fall on my face when walking down the street are signs of how estranged I feel in relation to the world around me. The amount of pain doesn't seem to depend on whether I'm in my own home or in a strange city. Actually, I've only been in a few places in my life where I've felt no pain. One of them is the mountains of Andalusia: the giddy scent of herbs and the jingle of the bells of the sheep herded by shepherds have always let me sink into a peaceful state of no pain.

Hallucinations are also part of the dissociative disorder. From my childhood, I remember continuous dreadful moments in the night when

I felt my body grow huge and then suddenly shrink and become almost non-existent. I'm lying on my bed and a tiny part of me soars above my body, expanding. When it's frighteningly big, it begins to force its way back into my body, and I'm terrified. In my body, it becomes tiny and begins to travel around. In another variation of this experience, the part of me that has soared above my body is thrown somewhere into space. It ends up on a track, flying from one end of the track to the other. On the track, I switch between being minute and gigantic.

My size can vary in the same way even when I'm walking down the street. When I suddenly experience my body as very small, the normal part of my personality has probably integrated with my child part. This can happen, for example, when I'm talking with a person who invokes the kind of fear in me that I felt as a child. While I'm walking down the street, "someone" may also take over my body and begin to move my hands and legs clumsily, as if learning to walk through me.

At times, I wish I were an animal, streaking down the street on four legs, roaring like a tiger or clawing like a cat. When the pressure in my body gets too great, the desire to release the stress in this way is activated somewhere in my reptilian brain. I do this when I'm alone, and it helps. As long as I can remember, I've felt like a tiger locked up in a cage when distressed. I claw and I hiss, but I can't get out.

A virtual seer beating on a shaman drum and offering guidance sometimes appears in my room, talking to me as if physically present. When I was younger, it seemed normal to live in a multidimensional world like this. Later, when I began to recognise fear and insecurity in myself, these phenomena started to terrify me. However, now I understand that they were a way for the different parts of my personality to tell about their existence. Originally, the voices came from outside my head. They gradually became part of me, turning into voices that were inside my mind and body.

At one time, my visual world was composed of geometrical patterns that hovered in the air, and I could use them to interpret people's feelings and intentions and the world around me. They flew into the air from different parts of my body, staying in my vision in the form of a network of patterns. Noticing the designs while talking to people made it hard for me to have an easy conversation. I learned to understand the patterns in a way that has meaning only for me. I'm not talking about a symbolic system that falls under a certain tradition, but an attempt to create an inner order for myself so that I could understand at least a small part of what people are signaling.

I believe that this synergy was created by the experiences I had when my father said one thing but meant another, when I sensed emotions that were in conflict with his words, and then he would behave in a totally unpredictable way. I remember staring at people with disbelief when I was younger, because I just couldn't understand what they had in mind. Often, the words they said didn't match the emotions they were sending out. Part of me was listening to them, and another part was watching their bodies. I felt that I couldn't trust anyone, since people lied intentionally by saying one thing while feeling another.

The geometrical patterns have been useful for me in observing my bodily states. I've drawn the parts of my body that feel or respond in different ways, giving them geometrical patterns in different colours; thus, I've improved my body awareness. The designs have a message for me: they tell me what the state of my body wants to convey to me at a given moment; it might be memories, or feeling bad or good about something that has just happened.

Physical pains and sensations often divide my body into a right and a left part. I used to wake up with my left side either numb or in pain from head to toe. When I was planning my first business and went to the public employment and business office, my right side kept turning my body so that only the left side was communicating with the official. Apparently, however, the official saw me as a whole person, since I got a startup grant! The body has its own way of responding to difficult situations, which can be confusing until you start to unravel the reactions gradually both on your own and with a therapist – and discover something rational in them.

I'm also very hypersensitive, which may be connected with traumatisation or some form of autism in me. On a bad day, I can't stand the sensation of any solid object close to me. For example, a table or a chair next to me makes me feel as if I were breaking apart. These solid ob-

The geometrical patterns have been useful for me in observing my bodily states. I've drawn the parts of my body that feel or respond in different ways, giving them geometrical patterns in different colours; thus, I've improved my body awareness.

jects increase the pressure on my nervous system, as though they were forcing themselves on me. In adolescence, I was afraid of all machines – even the copying machine: its buzzing made me feel sick.

ROUGH ON THE BODY

Maybe the most difficult effect of long-lasting traumatisation is the continuous state in which the body is either in submission or hyperaroused. For a long time I felt that I had only two choices: either to constantly have my body in an overactive state of fear or sink into submission.

When my daughter was in first grade, I often tried to walk the fifteen minutes it took me to get to the café to read the paper and have my first cup of coffee. Usually, the walk ended halfway with me sitting on a bench in a park, sliding somewhere. When I began to sink, I got a heavy feeling in my body as if a current of air was sucking my consciousness into a black tunnel. In no time at all, I fell asleep. After a few hours I woke up on the bench, wondering where the time had gone.

My submission may – or at least used to – last for weeks or even months. During those periods, I have no control over my body; I can't even move properly. However, my brain works, apart from the times when I'm in a dreamlike state. Sometimes the submission is only partial and affects just part of my body: for example, my right leg might not work. When I published my earlier book on traumatisation, I couldn't walk at all for a few weeks.

When my body is in the opposite state, hyperaroused, I may lose my hearing or my vision, which, of course, makes it almost impossible for me to work or find my way in the city. This has also happened to me during a meeting with a customer. My daughter absolutely hates it when I suddenly can't hear her anymore. She still believes that I'm just pretending.

Continuous states of strain, submission and pain take a heavy toll on the body. I've had my heart checked and numerous other tests taken. My symptoms seem serious. At times when I feel awful, I get seizures

186

as if I had epilepsy. My heart beats fast and I feel dizzy all the time. In our dissociation peer group, we often discuss whether I might not, after all, have some disease, or whether these symptoms are just caused by dissociation.

Fortunately, I haven't been diagnosed with any permanent disease. Still, the stress and pain from which my body has suffered for years have tired me physically. Sometimes, exhaustion descends on my body, and my face becomes old and tired in an instant. I must admit that I never knew how to take care of myself until I started going to therapy. Over and over, my therapist has emphasised the importance of routines in healing. Regular routines help me lead a more balanced life – something that is gentler for my body. Now that my worst, most extreme states have disappeared, I realise that persistently taking care of myself creates a basis for feeling better both physically and emotionally, and helps me gradually reduce my trauma-induced symptoms.

WORKING ON MEMORIES

The child in me said: "It's a secret." Another part of me asked: "Can your heart take it?" My inner protector told me that I couldn't reveal the secret, because I'd be accused and end up in prison: the police wouldn't believe me. Such a burden to bear: a secret so frightening that it could send you to prison. My father knew exactly how to control a small child's mind!

I've also dredged up messages that other members of my family have stored in my subconscious: "I can't blame my father, because he's a learned man and the breadwinner. He must be respected so that the family won't break up." "I'd rather kill myself than speak out." "I've already said three times that I'll kill you if you talk about it again." However, the warrior part of my personality has always thought: "Life is meant to be lived no matter how heavy or difficult it is."

I've worked on my memories ever since they appeared for the first time like a filmstrip in my mind. I've tried EMDR therapy (Eye Movement Desensitisation and Reprocessing) with the help of two different trauma therapists. With one of them, EMDR slammed my memories in front of me with a force that sent my body into spasms and gave me heart symptoms. Totally out of control, I was retraumatised. The groundwork had not been done, and I couldn't cope with the material connected with my traumatisation any better than as a child.

EMDR didn't give the desired results with the second therapist, either. Each one of my child parts tried to surface and tell its own story. I got some contact with them, but we didn't actually use the EMDR technique correctly, as the idea is to go through the traumatising scenes closely so that memories and emotions become integrated and give words to a new story. Therefore, I've removed EMDR from my tool kit for the time being.

Unravelling traumatic memories makes me ashamed. Part of me resists giving words to situations of abuse in particular. Some of my traumas were created so early in life that there aren't even words for the experiences.

The strongest sense of shame rises from the scenes which combine pleasure and pain. At one time, I externalised this experience by working as an s/m dominatrix. In other ways, too, sadomasochism seemed to suit my mindset: it was like a missing piece in experiencing my self in the "right" way. However, from a more comprehensive perspective, sadomasochism could not be connected with the pain/pleasure experience I'd had as a child. I was in control of sadomasochism and its special world when I was in my warrior personality state. In my child state, I'm a completely helpless victim – and admitting this really hurts.

Sadomasochism also nourished my need to be subjugated by reinforcing the only way I could feel accepted: when I'm punished I have the right to exist. In sadomasochism, I could also get in touch with the part of me that bears extreme hatred. I'm sure every deeply traumatised person can confirm that somewhere inside there's a desire to kill. When you've been humiliated, subjugated, punished and threatened often enough, the hate for the subjugator grows so intense that the desire to use violence emerges in you, too.

I've visited the fountain of hatred in my mind a few times, and don't want to do it ever again. It feels as if my head is full of pieces of a broken mirror – and extreme hate. I definitely don't feel like messing up my mind or reinforcing this state anymore. Nevertheless, I can imagine what people who have, for example, been driven to kill other people blindly have felt. I think I understand what people mean when they say: "Something just snapped in my head; I don't remember anything about what I did."

Can anyone or anything ever alleviate such agony in a person? Perhaps if the one who caused the damage would apologise, express regret, make up and assume the burden. This almost never happens, and, in reality, the traumatised person has to carry all the pain, hate, shame, blame and grief. And try to heal and become whole as best he or she can – and not seek revenge.

Sometimes I've vented my pain by cutting myself. The agony can be seen in the wounds in my skin and the blood that wells out. It's there the moment my memory returns and I realise I've cut myself in many places; when I grasp that there's a horror called agony living in me. Before the cutting takes place, I experience the world as threatening and myself as weird and lonely. In cutting, the different sides of the trauma become united, with me as the victim, facilitator and evil-doer at the same time. As the victim, I get revenge; the evil-doer is the target of my hate – that is, myself – and without the knife, I cannot cope with the agony. So I help myself.

When I started processing my trauma, I wrote:

When you talk to the pain, speak straight to its face.
Respect it. Speak from your heart. Let it flow
through your being.
It may move slowly. It may lead you to deep waters.
It may feel as if the oxygen is running out and you'll
never see light again.
Let it go and take you to light.
The pain knows the way home. Let it be your guide.

I feel that my heart has lost the battle concerning its right to live. But the part of me that functions pushes me to live, coming up with good reasons. In me, there's an agony that carries the part of my self that died once. Severe heart pain sometimes leads me to the experience of death. It doesn't stir my will to live; rather, it makes me want to die. It's an experience full of grief.

The great thing about trauma therapy is that you can return to it later, even after years. I feel that I'm not yet ready to admit all the things that have happened to me. I can write, have dreams, enter flashbacks and experience things intensely in my body, but I cannot yet face – what? I'll wait. Though some of my traumas have not yet been unravelled, I can enjoy the other advantages of integration, which include, for example, a decrease in flashbacks, the ability to be in the here and now, and the lessening of fears.

ON HATE

Situations at work, trauma memories and hate! Since I'm still unravelling my trauma memories, I haven't been able to trust that I can manage situations of conflict at work in a constructive way. Hate surfaces whenever I run into almost any kind of unsatisfactory situation. My needs have not been taken into consideration and – there we go! The fat is in the fire. I boil with anger and slam doors, my perception is clouded, I blurt accusations. I've left photo shoots, slamming doors. Dragged my photography equipment so that the bags have broken. I vent my hate for a few weeks and then try to sort things out. I start over from scratch.

Dealing with the hatred is therapeutic for the self in a way, but unfair to others. Through the process, you can refind your place in the world. To break away from the position of being a victim, you need the dynamic energy of hate. It's good that the hatred surfaces in concrete situations. When you've gone through this process a few times, you can start thinking about alternative ways of responding. It's important not to immediately judge yourself. The world can surely take the hate that a trauma survivor releases by blowing up a few times!

The accuser in me often blames me for allowing myself to be stained. It tries to make me a victim. My right foot, on the other hand, wants to kick my father in the balls, and such moments result in a nervous explosion and laughter. I'm angry for the right reason. You don't need to be afraid of this hate, but neither should you especially allow it to resurface. You need to take control of it and redirect it. Being angry must be re-introduced to the child parts as a positive thing, because anger is really frightening for them. The energy of hate is incredible, in fact! It's pure energy, the ability to defend yourself and others in the face of injustice.

Nevertheless, it can be problematic to do therapy work with the angry part of the personality, as it's not very keen on co-operating. It doesn't want to return to the flashbacks: it wants to be in the here and now. It appreciates strength, not weakness and being nice – the qualities the child parts often represent. It doesn't easily trust kind people such as therapists. Indeed, hate has often prevented me from having good moments in therapy.

I believe that there's some toughness and determination in me that will never disappear. At the moment, I recognise hate that is directed inwards in the pain my body produces. I didn't understand earlier that even having heart pains was a manifestation of hate. The inability to express hatred is often the reason for sudden dissociative disappearances. But hatred, when expressed for the right reason, helps you learn the difficult art of being in the here and now.

ON FEAR

My greatest source of fear has always been social situations and intimacy. Especially when I was young this fear steered my choices even to the extent that having the freedom to choose, at any given moment, where I would live and what I would do was my main mantra. To manage my life, I needed to be able to flee and choose anew. Building a family is the bravest thing I've ever done. I set out to study intimacy, asking whether I'd really be able to cope with it.

Each part of my personality has had its own way of fleeing its fears.

Most of the strategies have involved sudden disappearances; for example, I've found myself hitchhiking in the middle of the night to the other side of Europe. I've left work places for lunch without coming back. I've frequently ruined my earlier achievements just because I haven't been able to face an uncomfortable situation that might trigger shame. I resort to any behaviour that will turn the attention away from my fears.

At some point, I had to decide that I would start assuming responsibility for all the situations in my life. I wanted to treat people according to the values to which I subscribed. I wanted to learn to be empathetic and live in the here and now, because I realised that it was the only way I could be happy, especially in my most important relationships, with my daughter and my partner.

I've developed my work community skills by working in communal work premises. I try to be as open as possible. I observe the bodily states and thoughts that emerge in me when I'm being watched by others. Every day, I withdraw to discuss, together with my different parts, which thoughts about my inferiority have made me feel the worst. Could I name moments and situations that would prove that people also like me?

All of this is extremely difficult because, ever since childhood, I've believed that I'm stupid and never good enough. Instead of criticising aspects of my behaviour, people have judged me as a person. Without a clear sign of acceptance, I can't even feel present in a neutral way. But my body has gradually begun to relax in the presence of other people. The shaking, being petrified with horror, and the buzzing in my head have lessened, and I no longer watch and interpret people's expressions and bodily responses continuously.

I've realised that much of my strength is hidden in the fearful parts of my personality, so the courage and fear in me need to learn to understand each other. The better I understand myself and my various sides, the easier it is for me to be with people and believe that I can cope even if someone behaves unpredictably in relation to me. I have a boundless capacity for coping, if only I can come to terms with all the different sides of myself.

At the moments when I want to go through my fears consciously, getting to know them in the daytime in order to sleep well at night, I know that I'm on the road to facing my fears in a good way. The same applies to the time I take to watch magical fairy-tale films bubbling with hope on TV so that my inner child can smile for a while. It's new for me to understand that I'm enhancing my own security and that too much loneliness frightens my child parts, so I can't let them be alone for too long. I pay attention to my insecurity. I name my fears. Fear can be by my side, but no longer lead me.

I also realise that my various parts have a variety of useful skills. When I begin to be afraid of being left out and want to isolate myself, I give room to my "angry" part, which bears a memory of how to live with an I-don't-care attitude. Thus, I avoid falling into a chasm and can see the situation from a wider perspective. Maybe my interpretation of the scene wasn't a hundred per cent right to begin with; it's also good to have the possibility of correcting my point of view instead of fleeing. I no longer have the chain reaction of my angry part scolding and the accusing part looking down on my fearful child – resulting in the part of me that is ashamed being even more ashamed. This kind of chain reaction only leads to increased fear.

I'm still working on having my parts recognise and accept each other, as well as on remembering to ask their views in difficult situations. All through the day, I tell myself what I intend to do, what kind of changes can be expected and where I'm going to go. It's good to visualise new situations before they arise and, in particular, imagine how my different parts might react to them. Often, I go through the scenes with my parts, almost acting them out in my mind in advance: this is how the small child might experience these things and protect herself, while the aggressive adolescent might defend me this way, etc. The process is arduous, but it's often the only way to make sure that I can stay in the here and now. This applies to new and strange situations, in particular.

The crucial thing for me is that the various parts of my personality are no longer allowed to behave uncontrollably. I've noticed that they won't do that if I take charge of things and make it clear that there's nothing to be afraid of in a situation: if I can cope with people, shame and conflicts. It's demanding, but it's worth the effort.

I feel that I am, in many respects, already whole, myself. I see myself standing in the wind with my arms out, embracing everything that is in me. This means that all my diverse experiences of life – both good and bad – are a resource for me. And I am – enormous!

HELP FROM BODY THERAPIES

Of the various forms of body therapy, acupuncture and bonesetting have been the most useful ones for me, but only after the need for experiencing feelings rose from deep inside me. To dare to expose my body to the arousal of feelings, I first learned a range of methods through which I could manage my mind and various situations in daily life. I knew that I'd be able to live with whatever surfaced in me.

My fear of tension has been one of the hardest things to bear. By "tension" I mean a state in which my body begins to approach hyperarousal. It starts to itch, the blood circulates more quickly and the energy level rises. I panic, as the tension indicates that I'm about to face issues of insecurity. In acupuncture, I've been able to experience these states in a safe way. The practitioner is present and can regulate the arousal of my body with the needles.

There are still some spots in my body where secrets are hidden, such as the mid-point of the edge of my left shoulder blade. Treating it through acupuncture evoked a great deal of shame and numerous images from my primary school lessons during which I had been hit on the fingers with a pointer and suffered from bullying that resulted in me not being able to sit where I wanted. Needles stuck in my pelvis always evoked deep loneliness and neglect – or sitting in a dark storage cupboard where I was locked as a form of punishment.

One day, I met a former colleague who used to behave unpredictably. I felt uncomfortable meeting the person, but couldn't connect the feeling with the pain in my body. My pains used to follow a certain route through my body, ending up in my left ear and temple and causing a stabbing headache. In acupuncture this same route of pain was activated, and I learned that it's the so-called gallbladder meridian, which can

194   Artwork by Seija

hurt as a response to sudden changes in conditions. Not understanding why another person behaves unpredictably causes an inner conflict. This kind of insight helps integrate the separate worlds of my body and my emotions.

I've had similar body-mind experiences in connection with bone-setting. When my teenage daughter was out all night a few years ago, I was frightened and my left wrist, in particular, began to hurt. When my wrist was being treated, I heard my own mother talk about how she couldn't protect me. I was now going through the same thing with my own child. With this insight, I was able to start regulating the force of my anxiety so that it became manageable instead of just repeating the feelings of my own mother. The wrist pain disappeared.

I don't recommend body therapy for anyone who hasn't worked on body-mind information: in such a case, the flashbacks and parts of the personality can take possession of the consciousness too easily. When I was younger, I used to go to energy therapy, where I was told that there was not a drop of love in me. Whatever those words meant, they made me suspect for years that I was worse than the worst, good for nothing.

Discussion-oriented trauma psychotherapy, movement therapy and body therapies, as well as continuous self-treatment and self-observation, have taken me so far that I now recognise myself in the photos from my infancy or childhood. I recognise my expressions, and I remember the feelings connected with them and what my face felt like when I was, for example, confused. It's wonderful! I've read that I was wild and lively already as a small child. I believe it now. I can feel it. These kinds of changes that sound simple are great victories for me. So I do exist! Now I can confirm it.

ON ANCHORING

Anchoring is a simple technique to bring oneself back to the present. You need to study the technique to benefit from it.

The body of a traumatised person has been disgraced, the feelings stained and, in the worst case, the mind damaged. Where do you find an anchor that will help you stay in the body? I've managed to anchor myself to nature, as nature has always increased my well-being. When I had it toughest, I used to pack a rucksack and take my daughter and go hiking in the countryside; once, for example, we hiked from one mountain village to another in Andalusia in Southern Spain. With Nature breathing through me, I could breathe.

In daily life, the world of sounds is perhaps my best anchor. I stop everything, start listening to the sounds around me and describe them to myself: the loud noise of the car motor comes from outside; there's a drowsy buzzing in the room; I can hear nice piano music coming from the neighbour's place and steps that frighten me in the stairway. Such a listening exercise returns my brain to its normal state fairly quickly. I'm a very visual person and constantly use pictures in my work, so images and visual practices, which are often recommended for use in anchoring, don't work for me. I need a different kind of anchor.

COMING TO TERMS WITH EATING

Food and eating may have been the most unpleasant thing on my road to healing. They've been connected with people walking over and through me. Not eating has protected me. For a long time, it was like a black shield around me. I wanted to be open and wild and learn to enjoy food and to accept – what? Earlier, I felt that I'd accept rubbish: in the form of food and from people. I was anger, want, despair; there was a big grey area in my mental imagery. When I protected myself from external negative energy that was even more powerful than mine, I did it in ways that I could control. I could control my eating. This way, at least my self-disgust wouldn't keep growing. It was difficult to break this vicious circle and move on.

As I made headway with my therapy, I faced my eating problem on a deep level, connecting with it emotionally. I had experienced the world as a threat, but the decision to quit eating was a result of the thought that I should love the world – though I had no love for it. My incestuous father both loved and hated me. What does having to accept both pro-

197

tection and violation from the same person lead to? The contradiction destroys your ability to trust your sensations.

My aching stomach says: "Shame on you for complaining and being so dissatisfied!" I answer: "But it wasn't my fault!" My body has been stuck, unable to feel. Am I or am I not allowed to feel? Am I or am I not allowed to live?

I've made a documentary on my eating problems, and, while making it, I realised that my metabolism had already switched to a very slow rate when I was a child because my nervous system was constantly in fight or flight mode.

I used to be able to move on by thinking that I could do bigger things in future, but now I accept that, for the time being, it's better to stick to smaller things, maybe near home. To hold on to routines and familiar things. This allows me to bring myself quickly back to things like eating if the whirl of the trauma breaks me again. If I've been living for days on only water and coffee and have been unable to follow the habits of sensible eating I've prescribed for myself.

Only now, while writing this, have I reached a stage at which I communicate daily with my body concerning what kind of food it will receive. The food I can take isn't very diverse yet, but my first focus has been on making my bowels work and my stomach ache disappear and on getting at least some pleasure from eating. With a metabolism that functions, it's much easier to figure out, for example, which part of the pain and cloudiness in my head is caused by a problem of digestion and which part is caused by a traumatic emotional reaction that I haven't been able to identify yet. This way I can focus the treatment on the right things.

MOVING THE BODY

I've always been athletic, but the trauma and dissociation have had a negative effect on my physical activity, too. At times, I can practise and be good at a sport, but when the state of my personality changes – sometimes right in the middle of a match – I suddenly lose all my skill. It's really embarrassing, so I try to avoid getting into such situations.

I've found yoga useful, but only during the past few years – since I was able to find a better balance for my body in therapy. Yoga opens up and balances the body and helps you control it, but you must be careful that your emotional states and the different parts of your personality don't become too activated. This means that you have to stick to your own pace and listen to yourself and stop the movement right away if you start feeling too confused. Yoga is largely an activity where you work alone, and the same applies to strength training. The latter gives strength and poise to your being, usually without triggering the body.

Dance has always been the third important physical activity for me. One day, I'll find the courage to engage in partner dancing, but at the moment I get too confused by close physical interaction to be able to stay in the here and now. Nevertheless, I dance a lot alone, anywhere. Dancing helps me understand the emotions of the moment and brings me pleasure. It's a good form of self-expression. Through dancing, I can connect with my inner child, who always wants to rejoice and play now that I've made friends with her again.

Healing and the integration of my personality seem to progress through endless small steps that lead, suddenly, to a huge leap. Then I find myself unexpectedly on a new level of consciousness, with my brain no longer looking for the old ways of operating. Here's an example of one big change that happened recently.

I have a black tunnel that opens up from my chest to a space within me, and its mystery was solved when I noticed that I have certain anticipatory reactions in my body before my consciousness begins to slide into the tunnel and exhaustion takes over. For example, my hands begin to clench and my jaw tenses up. This means that I'm in a situation that evokes hate. My nervous system is ready to give up automatically, because the anger I expressed when I was traumatised as a child didn't bring about a change. When I began to recognise this hate response in me as an adult, I also noticed, at the same time, a voice in me saying: "It's not worth it". Earlier, I ignored the words, because, to survive, I had to dissociate, go away. When I have this kind of reaction now, it means that I haven't been able to give space or expression to my feelings and hopes.

This set of reactions is primed and ready to be activated in a matter of seconds if I meet, for example, an unpleasant person on the street. Not until I had completely deciphered this series of responses, triggered by the brain, could I begin to recognise it in daily situations and change my behaviour. This has clearly taken me to a new, lighter level of being.

Naturally, all this information has always been within me, for the body remembers. In movement therapy, I've begun to understand my body better. Movement therapy is a form of therapy where you dance out basic emotions such as shame, fear and hate; it has helped me pay attention to how the different emotions feel in my body. It's as if I were a child again, since childhood was the stage at which my connection to my body was broken. To move on to lightness and integration, it has been crucial for me to understand this whole palette: that is, the body-mind-emotion reactions.

When I understood that my trauma therapist really cared about me and believed my story, new thoughts about myself began to emerge. Maybe I, too, could be a loved person, someone whose well-being matters; a person for whom there's room to exist. Actually, the greatest resource behind my healing is that I now have one genuine experience of interaction in which I'm important and valuable: this has helped me raise my goal of a profoundly good life to a higher level. The greatest benefit of therapy is to be able to experience a secure relationship and to learn to trust another person.

OTHER PEOPLE AND ME

Therapy is the best forum for having healing experiences. A couple relationship cannot be the main forum for dealing with trauma: if you try it, your relationship will be on the skids. At the beginning of a new relationship, it's wise to go over the traumatic past of both partners, so that you know how demanding your communication will be in daily life. After that, however, the partners should focus on everything that knits them together and hold on to the things that make both of them

Artwork by Seija

Healing and the integration
of my personality seem to
progress through endless small
steps that lead, suddenly, to a
huge leap. Then I find myself
unexpectedly on a new level of
consciousness, with my brain no
longer looking for the old ways
of operating.

feel good.

If the partner of a traumatised person hasn't been neglected or reject-ed in some way as a child, he or she will quite certainly go through this experience in the relationship. It often happens that the partner seems to be doing the wrong thing and is rejected no matter what he or she tries. It might be wise for the partner also to go to some kind of therapy in order to have an idea about the nature of his or her own emotional blocks. This allows the couple to steer the relationship forward, past the most difficult pitfalls.

My worst experiences in relationships took place when my partner communicated poorly and hardly expressed his feelings. This was a practice that was familiar to me from my childhood family, so the be-haviour caused me to dissociate immediately. I removed myself from the situations. Fortunately, we managed to talk about it, and my partner eventually learned to observe his behaviour and even change it, com-pletely voluntarily. He understood what a negative effect it had on me.

When you've lived as a child in a close relationship of subjugation and control in relation to one of your parents, the control is transferred automatically to other relationships, too. You always assume that people cannot be trusted. But when you control other people, you also take on their worries and problems. When you add other people's psychological burdens to your own daily pain and anxiety, life becomes much more difficult.

To get rid of this burden, I began to pay attention to my emotional states in different situations. I noticed that when my partner came home and stepped through the door, instead of feeling good, I started to feel depressed, wanted to cry or came close to panicking, depending on the emotional state of my partner. I sometimes felt detached from myself for days without knowing where my sadness and anxiety came from. In-stead of facing my partner's states of mind by being present more open-ly, I fled from them by identifying with them.

Since it's been so easy for me to identify with the energies of other people, I have, at times, had to constantly study their thoughts and states of mind to be certain that being with those people would be safe for me. There was a time when I needed to contemplate in advance what would happen when I met someone, or what we'd talk about; otherwise, I wouldn't have been able to meet that person without fear. I still don't know whether you can really read another person's mind without your expectations colouring the interpretation.

After my recovery began, I continued to feel that I didn't even have the right to be and tread on earth. I practised long meditations during which I tried to become connected with the earth: that is, connected concretely with the physical earth and its energy. I asked for permission from "those who sustain and protect the earth" so that I could, for example, travel in some country.

Though this method sounds crazy, it has a symbolic meaning. There are times when a traumatised person has to build his or her life on symbols. In a way, they represent the real world with which you cannot otherwise connect. Naturally, you can get lost in the world of symbols, soaring on the wings of imagination forever. You can learn about the use of symbols, for example, from tribal nations that still use them to perform various rituals.

GUILT

Guilt is not just a thought or a feeling. It's a considerable obstacle that prevents energy from flowing in your body. Guilt and responsibility are companions. For a traumatised person they are both-and things: you get them as an "added bonus" of the trauma, but loaded with distorted feelings. Your mind reminds you: "Do something, you're responsible for everything, every single thing in the world. But if you do something, you'll be the one to blame for everything that goes wrong." This kind of thought pattern connects you to the world in a troubled and difficult way.

With progress in healing, I was finally able to feel that I wasn't the one to blame for everything. For a long time, I've been blamed for a mountain of things in my original family. I've been called the black sheep of the family, an exploiter. Proofs have been forged and lies told. Finally, I was lucky enough to encounter things that helped me realise that I was actually innocent. When this happened several times, I felt that the scales were finally about to be balanced.

With this balancing, I could start facing my real guilt. It was the beginning of redefining responsibility in my life: responsibility that concerns certain deeds of mine, not my whole personality and existence as an emissary of evil.

THE SHADOW OF DISAPPOINTMENT

The burden of disappointment that characterises my whole personality has been a big obstacle to my healing: I have simply been hurt too deeply. I've been disappointed at the lack of fairness in life and betrayed by the people who are the most important to me. It can't be helped anymore. I just have to hope that life will offer me something else. I've tried my best, and now I hope to get something back, in one form or another.

At present, I believe that life will carry you, but you have to work hard for the good things. You have to think, so that the brain cements new connections in your nerve cells. At first, you have only hope to rely on. Eventually new, positive thoughts begin to feel like something, and you start waking up feeling grateful in the morning. You choose things that maintain your well-being, and you feel good more and more often. When the world starts to reflect back joy and warmth, the worst is over.

The trick may be to realise that you need to quit feeling powerless. You need to take responsibility for everything in life: friendships, family, your health, and, as much as possible, your livelihood. With responsibility, you get back your power.

Energy that is bound to a trauma can be released and taken into free use; I've come a long way in learning how to use that energy. I'm living my life to the full, in the here and now. The trauma is, in a way, a gateway to freedom and away from illusions. If you go through the trauma-induced illusions bravely and patiently with the help of consciousness development, you will emerge victorious.

HEALING!

I'm on my way to healing, and I feel secure. I feel part of the world, at least for the time being. I've been heard, seen and taken into consideration. My experiences have been given words and meaning. In addition to therapy, I've benefited from meeting others who struggle with dissociative disorders. I understand them instantly; for once, I feel that I'm similar to other people and normal! This book project has been part of my healing and vital for me. I'm no longer as afraid of myself as earlier.

With therapy, a new lightness has gradually found me, giving me hope that this process can create room for new, more positive feelings such as joy and happiness. That one day I may no longer need to be constantly aware of my trauma – a difficult state that is both exhausting and draining.

I'm now moving on to such lightness; I'm about to heal and recognise myself as one self. It's even been hard to write about those approximately fifty difficult years, because the change is so real. After all this, I've started wondering why it's so difficult to heal without proper assistance if your mind is traumatised and dissociative. Why is help not provided for all those in need?

For years, I've described different states of mind and situations to therapists; I've drawn them and written about them, figuring out on the basis of calendar notes when they might occur. When dissociation begins to intensify in me, I try to take charge of my brain by listening to and verbalising the sounds around me. Nevertheless, the road has been long and difficult. I've relied on hope, determination and persistence; I've been determined to win my life back.

CLOSING WORDS!

Never give up! No one will save you if you don't do it yourself. Use all the available means. You will find and get help! Miracles happen. Find a peer group. It takes time to heal, but, at the same time, you will write history through your own story of healing. One day, it will be perfectly normal to have dissociative disorders diagnosed and treated. Together with our therapists, we're building up a new practice.

Artwork by Carita

EPILOGUE

THE PEER GROUP: A SPIRITUAL HOME

Anssi Leikola

I have often been sceptical about technology. However, I have already had to give in and change my basic views many times in my life, and I am happy to do so again now. It is amazing how the Internet and the digital world shape the social terrain of our species, both for good and for bad. It seems that it is precisely those who are suffering from serious attachment traumas who benefit most from the Internet, as they often believe that there is no-one like them in the world, and, even if they know that there are others, they often tend to avoid meeting peers face to face, not to mention coming out of the closet with the dissociative disorder. It would be interesting to conduct a socio-anthropological study of this subject. How is a tribal culture created and how does it grow among people who have earlier been isolated or without a group of their own and a sense of belonging?

Since the Finnish version of this book was published in 2016, I have had the opportunity to get to know the other authors, and today we form a growing peer community. I feel that I have again reached a new phase in life, as I have, for the first time, a community of which I feel that I am automatically a part. It is extraordinary that precisely people who have been extremely insecure in their own lives have formed a community in which I feel so incredibly secure. It says everything essential about the extent of identification and the quality of sharing in this group. At the same time, it is also an amazing sign of the possibilities that social media and the digital sphere offer us today. The world is indeed changing: people can no longer be controlled and their doings regulated from above in the same way as earlier. We are now seeing completely new ways of meeting, possibilities and also influence at the grassroots level!

One of the subjects in which I have been the most interested has been the impact of traumatisation and structural dissociation on one's social engagement. It is illuminating to observe the multitude of ways in which these processes can shape the nervous mechanisms of social engagement systems and the way we cling to the environment (e.g., Järvilehto, 1994). Childhood traumatisation hampers one's ability to share experiences, making healing complex in various, at times surprising but still understandable, ways. Allusions connected with this impact of traumatisation and conveyed in therapeutic meetings often give access to significant information about the past. I believe that I have something special to offer as concerns these issues, because my personal history is so untypical in relation to what we call "social life". Most probably, this provides me with a special opportunity of looking at these issues in a way of my own – in a way that already seems to have benefited many traumatised people. I may also be free of the kind of (social) weight connected with the tradition of psychiatry that limits the range of possible observations in advance.

To get to this point, all of us writers have done an enormous amount of mental work, combined with cooperation. There are two things that we no longer need to give up: the sense of having influence and the sense of being part of a community. We inspire each other. Our group is characterised by a variety of talents and the capacity to create the most diverse channels in order to attain our goals; we have the same mission, and it has raised each of us to a new level. Thus we reach, both as individuals and as a group, ever higher stages in Pierre Janet's hierarchy of action tendencies: long-term, creative and ever-evolving deeds. Everyone can participate in our activities to the extent that his or her situation, condition and capacities allow. You are guaranteed to find encouragement.

We do not know whether there are projects elsewhere in the world in which patients with dissociative disorders have, as a group, published or presented their experiences in other ways, organised peer activities or started communities. As far as we are aware, no such projects exist yet. In any case, we are convinced that other groups will be started, and we hope to have contact with them. We are interested in sharing experiences and will gladly assist in launching group activities. Our experiences are so thrilling, touching and, above all, healing that we hope to be able to share them internationally.

One of the recent signs of the power of change was how our book caught on at the national Mental Health Fair in Finland in the autumn of 2016. For example, the venue did not have enough seats for everyone who wanted to come and listen to us. Traumatisation and dissociation will be one of the main themes of the 2017 fair as well.

At present, we are living evidence of how belonging to a secure peer community affects one's self-esteem. The effect can even be compared to the impact of successful trauma psychotherapy. We are developing a model for a community that will be sufficiently safe for patients with dissociative disorders; it will contain a proper amount of both consistency and flexibility. We aim at making this model, The Coequal Dissociation Community – Healing Tribe, available to the world as a Finnish innovation.

We know our worth and we know that our number will grow, because we can meet our peers in an appreciative and sympathetic way. We are ready, responsive and capable of cooperation with all those who share our main objective of improving the position of traumatised people. But we want to be treated in the same way: equally and with respect. We have learned that this is an effective form of cooperation that allows everyone to win. This is an invitation.

It is time to recognise all the capacity that can be found in psychiatric patients who are recovering. We are not satisfied with only rehabilitation work offered to those recovering from mental illness: we want to attain our best potential. It seems that sharing recovery experiences will enable many of us to provide for ourselves, and our goal is to create such opportunities for our peers as well. We can participate in discussions in society and identify ourselves as a force for change. We categorically reject the patronising and passive position almost automatically imposed on psychiatric patients. We are humble enough to understand what huge and laborious things cultural changes are; we know that we will be up against, for example, an element that can be labelled "defence of acquired benefits", but we are also proud enough to recognise that we, as a group, are a skilful and active opinion leader.

We not only have the delight but also the moral obligation to help, as best we can, our peers who are working their way toward liberation from their traumas, with each one at a different point on their journey. We want to share, mediate and promote the good things that we have encountered on our own paths. Trust creates trust. This kind of positive cycle is especially needed in the present global political situation, where many phenomena that arouse insecurity are shaking nations. Now, in 2017, several leading figures on the international stage are giving extremely unfortunate and harmful examples through behaviour that produces attachment traumas.

Psychiatry is at present strongly medication-oriented, which makes me feel that the focus is too often on numbing and offering submission rather than a cure to patients. This also means that valuable stories are at risk of being buried.

As it happens, at the same time I have been giving the finishing touches to this introduction, UN Special Rapporteur Dainius Pūras, a Lithuanian professor of psychiatry, has published a report highlighting numerous extremely important goals from the point of view of mental health, recognising the vast failures that have become a chronic problem in present-day psychiatry. He suggests that we should aim at a revolution that would make human rights the basis of psychiatry! The report contains a variety of views with which I agree wholeheartedly, as well as ambitious objectives that are very close to, if not identical with, my own mission (Pūras, 2017). I warmly recommend the report to anyone who wonders about the present situation of psychiatry. It contains an incredible number of compact, felicitous and also painful observations on the problems of psychiatry and on the direction in which this professional field of mine should be advanced. Such a great, welcome and brave report! It reminds me of the words of the former president of Finland, J. K. Paasikivi, who said: "Recognising the facts is the beginning of all wisdom".

If psychiatry really could be based on human rights, it would be both much safer and more cost-effective! It is important that we can and are allowed to have dreams.

It is so easy to be cynical and pessimistic as concerns traumatisation and the possibility of recovering from it. This is where we are needed as a group, a community – as an example of a unique thought collective.

This is a good place to quote Kerstin Uvnäs-Moberg's wise words: "Positive social contacts of any kind increase oxytocin release" and "When oxytocin prevails, a sense of community and trust is created and therefore a greater understanding of others and thus openness to negotiation and change" (Uvnäs Moberg, 2009, pp. 154-155). The experiences we have had in our community confirm these results of the research on oxytocin!

Healing from dissociative disorders leads to dramatic personal changes that are reflected in all spheres of life. The fundamental characteristics of the human species include the telling and sharing of stories, and when this natural need is dammed up for decades, we get a force of nature that even has a biological basis. Thus, the narratives of those who have recovered from traumatisation contain incredible power when they are finally released and publicly shared.

When this force is no longer constrained but becomes integrated with new technological innovations, unprecedented meetings with peers and a sense of community, and experience in helping one's peers in critical life situations, we will enter new landscapes – the kind no-one has ever seen. Then, life will no longer be the same: it will have changed permanently into something better.

BIBLIOGRAPHY

For Anssi Leikola's texts on pages 16 to 53 and pages 208 to 212.

Boon, S., Steele, K., & Van der Hart, O. (2011). *Coping with Trauma-Related Dissociation. Skills Training for Patients and Therapists.* W. W. Norton & Company: New York, London.

Caspi, A., Sugden, K., Moffitt, T. E., Taylor, A., Craig, I. W. , Harrington, H., McClay, J., Mill, J., Martin, J., Braithwaite, A., & Poulton, R. (2003). Influence of Life Stress on Depression: Moderation by a Polymorphism in the 5-HTT Gene. *Science, 301*(5631), 386-389.

Diseth, T. (2005). Dissociation in children and adolescents as reaction to trauma – An overview of conceptual issues and neurobiological factors. *Nordic Journal of Psychiatry, 59*(2), 79-91.

Edelman, G., & Tononi, G. (2000). *A Universe of Consciousness. How Matter Becomes Imagination.* Basic Books: New York.

Ehling, T., Nijenhuis, R. R. S., & Krikke, A. (2007). Volume of discrete brain structures in complex dissociative disorders. Preliminary findings. *Progress in Brain Research*, 167, 307-310.

Ellenberger, H. F. (1970). *The Discovery of the Unconscious.* The History and Evolution of Dynamic Psychiatry. Basic Books: New York.

Fleck, L. (1979). *Genesis and Development of a Scientific Fact (Entstehung und Entwicklung einer wissenschaftlichen Tatsache).* University of Chicago Press: Chicago and London.

Haavisto, P. (2011). *Anna mun kaikki kestää. Sovinnon kirja* [Go on, Let Me Have it. A Book of Reconciliation]. WSOY: Helsinki.

Hietala, J., Heinimaa, M., & Suvisaari, J. (2015). Tutkimus on muuttanut käsitystämme psykooseista [Research Has Changed Our View of Psychoses]. *Duodecim*, 131(22), 2117-2124.

Husserl, E. (2006). Uudistuminen yksilöeettisenä kysymyksenä [Renewal as a Problem in Individual Ethics] in S. Heinämaa (Ed.), *Uudistuminen ja ihmisyys: luentoja ja esseitä* [Renewal and Humanity: Lectures and Essays]. Tutkijaliitto, Helsinki.

Huttunen, M. O. & Leikola, A. J. (2017). *Traumatisoivat kokemukset ja masennus* [Traumatic Experiences and Depression]. In O. Kampman, T. Heiskanen, M. Holi, M. O. Huttunen, & J. Tuulari (Eds.), Masennus [Depression] (pp. 255-262). Kustannus Oy Duodecim: Helsinki.

Järvilehto, T. (1994). *Ihminen ja ihmisen ympäristö. Systeemisen psykologian perusteet* [Human Beings and Their Environment. Fundamentals of Systemic Psychology]. Pohjoinen: Oulu.

Kivimäki, V. (2013). *Murtuneet mielet. Taistelu suomalaissotilaiden hermoista 1939–1945* [Broken Minds. Fighting over the Nerves of Finnish Soldiers 1939–1945]. WSOY: Helsinki. (Based on Kiviniemi's doctoral thesis "Battled Nerves: Finnish Soldiers' War Experience, Trauma and Military Psychiatry, 1941–1944". Åbo Akademi: Turku, 2013).

Leikola, A. (2014). *Katkennut totuus* [The Broken Truth]. Prometheus kustannus: Helsinki.

Leikola, A., Mäkelä, J., & Punkanen, M. (2016). Polyvagaalinen teoria ja emotionaalinen trauma [The Polyvagal Theory and Emotional Trauma]. *Duodecim*, 132(1), 55-61.

Nijenhuis, E. R. S. (2015 & 2017). *Trinity of Trauma. Ignorance, Fragility and Control. Vols. I-III.* Vandenhoeck & Ruprecht: Göttingen.

Ogden, P., Minton, K., & Pain, C. (2006). *Trauma and Body. A Sensorimotor Approach to Psychotherapy.* W. W. Norton & Company: New York, London.

Panksepp, J. (1998). *Affective Neuroscience. The Foundations of Human and Animal Emotions.* Oxford University Press: New York, Oxford.

Poijula, S., Leikola, A., & Suokas-Cunliffe, A. (2015). Traumapsykoterapiat [Trauma psychotherapies]. In M. Huttunen & H. Kalska (Eds.): *Psykoterapiat,* 3rd edition [Psychotherapies]. Kustannus Oy Duodecim: Helsinki.

Porges, S. W. (2011). *The Polyvagal Theory. Neurophysiological Foundations of Emotions, Attachment Communication and Self-Regulation.* W.W. Norton & Company: New York, London.

Pūras, D. (2017). Report of the Special Rapporteur on the right of everyone to the enjoyment of the highest attainable standard of physical and mental health. Human Rights Council, Thirty-fifth session, 6-23 June, 2017. United Nations A/HRC/35/21.

Rayner, A., & Järvilehto, T. (2008). From Dichotomy to Inclusionality: A Transformational Understanding of Organism-Environment Relationships and the Evolution of Human Consciousness. *Journal of Transfigural Mathematics*, 1(2), 67-82.

Read, J., Fosse, R., Moskowitz, A., & Perry, B. (2014). Traumagenic neurodevelopmental model of psychosis. *Neuropsychiatry*, 4(1), 65-79.

Reinders, A. A. T. S., Nijenhuis, E. R. S., Quak, J., Korf, J., Haaksma, J., Paans, A. M. J., Willemsen, A. T. M., & Den Boer, J. A. (2006). Psychobiological Characteristics of Dissociative Identity Disorder: A Symptom Provocation Study. *Biological Psychiatry*, 60, 730-740.

Rissanen, P. (2015). *Toivoton tapaus? Autoetnografia sairastumisesta ja kuntoutumisesta* [A Hopeless Case? An Autoethnography of Falling Mentally Ill and Rehabilitation]. Kuntoutussäätiö: Helsinki.

Schlumpf, Y. R., Reinders, A. A. T. S., Nijenhuis, E. R. S., Luechinger, R., Van Osch, J. P., & Jäncke, L. (2014). Dissociative part-dependent resting-state activity in dissociative identity disorder: A controlled fMRI perfusion study. *PLOS ONE*, 9(6). Retrieved from PLOS ONE (e98795).

Schäfer, I., Ross, C. A., & Read, J. (2008). Childhood trauma in psychotic and dissociative disorders. In A. Moskowitz, I. Schäfer, & M. J. Dorahy (Eds.), *Psychosis, Trauma and Dissociation. Emerging Perspectives on Severe Psychopathology* (pp. 137-150). Wiley–Blackwell: Chichester (UK), Hoboken, NJ, (US).

Siwecka, S. (2011). Genesis and development of the "medical fact". Thought style and scientific evidence in the epistemology of Ludwik Fleck. *Dialogues in Philosophy, Mental and Neuro Sciences*, 4(2), 37-39.

Steele, K., Van der Hart, O., & Nijenhuis, E. R. S. (2001). *Dependency in the Treatment of Posttraumatic Stress Disorder and Dissociative Disorders. Journal of Trauma and Dissociation*, 2(4), 79-116.

Steele, K., Van der Hart, O., & Nijenhuis, E. R. S. (2005). Phase-Oriented Treatment of Structural Dissociation in Complex Traumatization: Overcoming Trauma-Related Phobias. Journal of Trauma & Dissociation, 6, 11-53.

Stern, D. (2004). *The Present Moment in Psychotherapy and Everyday Life*. W. W. Norton & Company: New York, London.

Uvnäs Moberg, K. (2009). *The Hormone of Closeness. The role of oxytocin in relationships*. Pinter & Martin Limited: London.

Van der Hart, O., Nijenhuis, E. R. S., Steele, K., & Brown, D. (2004). Trauma-related dissociation. Conceptual clarity lost and found. *Australian and New Zealand Journal of Psychiatry*, 38, 906-914.

Van der Hart, O., Nijenhuis, E. R. S., & Steele, K. (2006). *The Haunted Self. Structural Dissociation and Treatment of Chronic Traumatization*. W. W. Norton & Company: New York.

Van der Hart, O. & Witztum, E. (2008). Dissociative psychosis: Clinical and theoretical aspects. In A. Moskowitz, I. Schäfer, & M. J. Dorahy (Eds.), *Psychosis, Trauma and Dissociation: Emerging Perspectives on Severe Psychopathology* (pp. 257-269). Wiley–Blackwell: Chichester (UK), Hoboken, NJ (US)

Van der Kolk, B. A. & Van der Hart, O. (1989). Pierre Janet and the Breakdown of Adaptation in Psychological Trauma. *American Journal of Psychiatry*, 146(12), 1530-1540.

Westö, K. (2013). *Kangastus 38* [Mirage 38]. Otava: Helsinki.

For further information on our project
and how to order books,
please visit:
www.fivesurvivors.com
or contact us
contact@fivesurvivors.com

We want to hear from you!